Anonymous

Descriptive Pamphlet of Hillsborough County, Florida

Anonymous

Descriptive Pamphlet of Hillsborough County, Florida

ISBN/EAN: 9783337083069

Printed in Europe, USA, Canada, Australia, Japan

Cover: Foto ©ninafisch / pixelio.de

More available books at **www.hansebooks.com**

DESCRIPTIVE PAMPHLET OF
HILLSBOROUGH COUNTY
WITH NUMEROUS ENGRAVINGS AND MAPS

HILLSBOROUGH COUNTY REAL ESTATE AGENCY.
TAMPA, FLA.

DESCRIPTIVE PAMPHLET OF

HILLSBOROUGH COUNTY,

FLORIDA,

WITH NUMEROUS MAPS, ENGRAVINGS, ETC.

1885.

PUBLISHED BY THE

HILLSBOROUGH COUNTY REAL ESTATE AGENCY,

TAMPA, FLORIDA.

ILLUSTRATED AND PRINTED FOR THE
※ HILLSBOROUGH COUNTY ※
REAL ESTATE AGENCY,
— BY —
THE ✳ SOUTH ✳ PUBLISHING ✳ COMPANY,
NO. 95 WARREN STREET, NEW YORK.

COPYRIGHT, 1885, BY THE HILLSBOROUGH COUNTY REAL ESTATE AGENCY.

ORGANIZATION.

BOARD OF DIRECTORS

HON. JOHN T. LESLEY,   WM. B. HENDERSON,   S. A. JONES.

OFFICERS:

JOHN T. LESLEY, President.   LAWSON CHASE, Secretary.
S. A. JONES, General Manager.   G. T. CHAMBERLAIN, Treasurer.

MEMBERS.

Stephen M. Sparkman, Esq., Phil. H. Collins, Wm. B. Henderson, T. C. Tallaferro, Bank of Tampa; Geo. B. Sparkman, Esq., John T. Lesley, S. A. Jones, A. J. Knight, G. T. Chamberlain, Lawson Chase, W. A. Givens and T. K. Spencer, of Tampa, Fla.; P. E. Warburton, of Acton, Fla.; C. L. Mitchell, Commissioner of Lands, Tallahassee, Fla.; Samuel N. Honaker, of Abingdon, Va.

REFERENCES:

Joseph F. Norris, Charleston, S. C.; Hon. S. F. Fleharty, Antelopeville, Neb.; Hon. S. J. A. Frazier, Chattanooga, Tenn.; Hon. Francis Colton, Galesburg, Ill.; Rev. Chas. Foster Garratt, Little Few Grange, Extone, Oxon., England; O. H. Platt, Esq., Hyde Park, Chicago, Ill.; Ex-Governor Albinus Nance, Osceola, Neb.; Hon. E. H. Marvill, Stromburg, Neb.; Dr. Sol. Smith, Denver City, Col.; Jas. L. Gilbert, Sulphur Springs, Texas; John A. Middleton, President Trader's Bank, Shelbyville, Ky.; John C. Williams, Detroit, Mich.; Hon. Jerome F. Chase, Florence, S. C.; S. Johnson, Newton, Ill.

ADDRESS ALL COMMUNICATIONS TO THE

HILLSBOROUGH ◊ COUNTY ◊ REAL ◊ ESTATE ◊ AGENCY,

Box 104,

TAMPA, FLORIDA.

A. S. LENFESTEY,

FURNITURE DEALER

— AND —

UNDERTAKER.

I can guarantee prices on all grades of furniture as low (if not lower) freights considered, as in any market in the United States. Stock comprises every thing that can be called for in the furniture line. Parties intending to settle will save money by selling their old furniture, thereby saving expense of packing, freights, and risk of breakage while in transit.

We are prepared to attend to the last honors that friends can wish for departed ones; but as no one comes to Florida to die, we wish to merely announce the fact that this is part of our business.

TAMPA, FLORIDA.

INDEX OF CONTENTS.

	PAGE.
Introduction,	7
General Description of County,	11
General Description of Tampa,	23
General Description of Plant City.	33
General Description of other Places and Post Offices in County,	33
Soil,	35
Fruit Growing.	37
Railroads,	41
Fish,	43
Timber,	45
Cattle Raising.	49
Tampa Bay.	54
Early Vegetables.	57
School System,	59
Sponge Trade.	61
Climate and Health.	63
Conclusion.	65
Appendix.	67

JOHN JACKSON,

— DEALER IN —

GENERAL MERCHANDISE.

One of the oldest and most reliable houses in Tampa. Carries a heavy line of

GROCERIES,

Dry Goods & General Furnishing Goods.

AGENT FOR HOME MEAL FERTILIZER.

LEONARDI'S OINTMENT.

The curative properties of this Ointment are truly wonderful, astounding not only the patient and friends, but also the intelligent physician, by its almost miraculous cures of some of the most obstinate cases of Tetter, Ringworm and Itching Piles, on record. Below we give some extracts from testimonials:

I was cured of Tetter of nineteen years' standing, by three applications of Leonardi's Ointment—Thomas P. Kennedy, Tampa, Fla. Less than one box of Leonardi's Ointment cured me of Tetter, of seventeen years' standing—Jno. L. Taylor, Jr., Member of Florida Legislature from Hillsborough county. One box of Leonardi's Ointment cured me of an aggravated case of Tetter of twenty-seven years—Lew E. Sparkman, Sparkman, Fla. I had Tetter for three years and was cured with Leonardi's Ointment—G. B. Sparkman, Ex-Mayor, Tampa, Fla.

We are now putting up two sizes—50 cents and 75 cents.

Agencies: S. R. Van Duzer, 35 Barclay St., New York; G. R. Finlay & Co., and J. L. Lyons & Co., New Orleans.

— PREPARED ONLY BY —

S. B. LEONARDI & CO.,

DRUGGISTS,

TAMPA, FLORIDA.

INTRODUCTION.

The changes which Time, with his majestic and enchanting wand, has wrought, can be no more fully realized and understood than when we contemplate that section of country whose verdure and beauty in landscape and water scenery called forth the admiration and rejoicings of Hernando DeSoto, as he, with his followers, sailed up the waters of Tampa Bay in the budding spring time of 1569. With good reason did he gaze in bewildered astonishment and wonder at the freshness and vigor of its vegetation and the bloom and blossom of its flowers. It was with a just and not a mistaken pride that he meditated upon the glory and renown which would flow to his beloved King and Queen, as the possessors of such a land, when he stepped upon the sandy shores and planted, for the first time, deep in the fertile soil, the staff which spread to the genial breezes of the sunny clime the silken folds of the flag of Spain.

Who can even faintly imagine the sensations and sentiments which would swell the breast and fill the soul of that ancient explorer if, through Divine power, the breath of life should be once more breathed into the mouldering remains, and in life and flesh he should visit again this same beautiful section in its present state of development, and view from the highest attainable pinnacle the wonderful impressions and changes which Time, aided by the progressive spirit of the Americans of to-day, has stamped upon its every feature! Great indeed have been the changes! He would find that the Red man, with his wigwams, his bows and arrows, his war-whoops and paints, has betaken himself to other parts and other climes. He would see that instead of the rude huts of these aborigines, scattered here and there, comfortable houses and elegant mansions, embellished with all the architectural skill, and fitted with all the comforts and conveniences of the modern day, have been erected in the shady groves, the thriving villages and the flourishing towns of this prosperous country. He would note that where once, only the light, shadowy canoe could be seen skimming along the surface of the blue waters, now, hundreds of sail-boats and many large and elegant steamers, laden with the rich products of the soil, and freighted with human lives, plow these waters daily and hourly. He would see, instead of the indistinct trail over which the stealthy hunter lightly threaded his way through the great forest, whose silence was broken only by an occasional war-whoop or the hoot of

MORRISON & PACKWOOD,

JOBBERS AND RETAILERS OF

HARDWARE STOVES AND TIN WARE

AGENTS
— FOR —

Olliver Chilled Plow. Kalamazoo Cultivator.

S. L. ALLEN PLANET. JR.. TOOLS.

CROCKERY AND LAMPS.

WOOD, WILLOW AND GLASS WARE.

AGRICULTURAL IMPLEMENTS.

HOES. Rakes. Scythes. SHOVELS AND SPADES. Boats. BROOMS AND BARROWS.

ICE CREAM FREEZERS. Coolers. Water Filters. REFRIGERATORS. PLOWS.

TAMPA
FLA.

Double Store under
OPERA HOUSE.

If you want a home in Florida apply to this Agency. Facilities unsurpassed by any in the State.

MONEY LOANERS OR BORROWERS,

LAND

Sellers or Buyers will find it to their interest to read what is said on page 70 by the

HILLSBOROUGH COUNTY REAL ESTATE AGENCY.

D. S. MACFARLANE.   H. E. CLEAVELAND.

MACFARLANE & CLEAVELAND,
Wholesale & Retail dealers in

BOOTS, SHOES AND SLIPPERS.
Franklin Street, opposite Court House, Tampa, Fla.

the owl, the iron track, over which the daily train, bearing the commerce of the world and the tourist of the colder climes, comes bounding, waking the echoes of the most distant regions, as it safely speeds on to their destination the hundreds who have availed themselves of its accommodation. In all around he would see and acknowledge that an enlightened civilization, with all of its natural outgrowths and a Divine Christianity, with all its benign influences, had played well their parts. And as he contemplated all these changes, instinctively and irresistibly would he contrast the present condition and occupation of the white man with that of the first one who visited these shores, and whom he found a prisoner of the Indians upon his arrival here. Though somewhat shrouded in mystery, yet it is a fact that Hernando DeSoto was not the first white man to land in Florida. "A youth to fortune and to fame unknown," filled with the spirit of adventure and discovery which characterized that era of the world's history, sailed up the beautiful waters of Tampa Bay, and, like many others since then, even down to the present day, was so enraptured with the salubrity of the climate, the fertility of the soil and the prospect of an orange grove that he declined to journey further with his companions and allowed them to set sail without him. His life was one grand holiday, and all with him and the Indians was as "salubrious" as the climate, until it was discovered that he was wooing the daughter of the chief of the tribe. He was then made prisoner, and after trial condemned to guard and keep watch in the future over the graves of those who had gone on to enjoy the chase on the happy hunting grounds in the Beyond, and so DeSoto found him. Here we must drop our Spanish discoverer, for 't would tire the reader for us to follow him through all his amazements and peculiar experiences, his final settlement and abode in this prosperous country, his second death and burial, for the country is our subject and he is only an incident.

GENERAL DESCRIPTION OF COUNTY.

The section of which we speak you have no doubt already recognized; at any rate, it is now known as Hillsborough county, and we invite and earnestly solicit your attention while we set forth its claims to the world, in frankness and in truth.

Having its boundaries defined on the west by the briny waters of the Gulf of Mexico, it extends from 27 deg. 20 min. to 28 deg. 50 min. north latitude, and from 82 deg. to 82 deg. 50 min. west longitude from Greenwich. Its sister counties are Hernando, Polk and Manatee; Hernando bounding it on the north, Polk on the east and Manatee on the south. Its boundary lines meet each other at right angles, and its shape would be that of a rectangle were it not for the coast line, which is very irregular and which is indented from north to south with many small estuaries and bayous. It is situated on the western coast of the Florida peninsula, as you know, and contains within its limits 852,480 acres, taking into count both its land and water surface. It is divided into forty-eight townships, each presumed to be six miles square, at which calculation the county would be thirty-six miles in length and forty-eight miles in width. Nature, in her freaks of generosity and munificence, could certainly have bestowed but little more upon this section for the happiness and enjoyment of its inhabitants. She has given it a Bay which extends inland to such a distance that it becomes almost land-locked, thus furnishing one of the most inviting harbors, accessible to the thousand vessels engaged in the Gulf trade, and which come laden with the rich merchandise of the world. And it takes no wizard or prophet to clearly perceive that Tampa Bay, by virtue of its geographical position and natural advantages, is soon to become the connecting link between the freighted cars of the railroads of the North and the palatial vessels of the outer deep, which will carry on the fast growing commerce with the nationalities of Central and South America and the islands of the sea. But for the present we have premised sufficiently concerning this magnificent Bay, which adds so materially to Florida's facilities for communicating with the remainder of the world, and which, with a reasonable appropriation by Congress, can and will be made the best and most desirable haven for the many ships which now proudly plow the waters of the Gulf. Then, too, she has given us a climate of which we could not complain if we would. Far enough South to be free from the snow and ice and chilling blast of the North, and fanned by the gentle zephyrs and Australian breezes which come wafted from the cooling waters of the Bay and Gulf, we are in the continual enjoyment of the most salubrious and equable climate. And in this connection we may, with propriety and fitness, quote from the "Statisti-

Report on the mortality in the army, compiled from the records of the Surgeon General's Office:

CLIMATE.

"The climate of Florida is remarkably equable and proverbially agreeable, being subject to fewer atmospheric variations, and in its thermometric ranges much less than any other part of the United States, except a portion of the coast of California." And again, in a few passages further down, we find: "The mean annual temperature of Augusta, Ga., is nearly eight degrees, and of Fort Gibson, Ark., upwards of ten degrees lower than at Tampa, yet in both these places the mean summer temperature is higher than at Fort Brooke" (Tampa); and it further states that such facts are positively shown by meteorological statistics on file in that bureau. We can state, unqualifiedly and with truthfulness, that in the summer months we suffer much less from the heat than those who dwell in the more northerly climes, which fact can be readily seen and appreciated by a comparison of the number of sunstrokes which daily occur in the Northern cities and the rare, rare ones in our section. In fact, so delightful and fascinating is our climate to our Northern friends that some of them have, notwithstanding the real fertility of our soil and the black rankness of our vegetation, remarked that we sell the climate and throw in the land. Such remarks are intended as no depreciation of our soil, but only as a very emphatic manner of expressing their honest appreciation of our balmy air and sunny clime. They spring from the same source as did the opening sentence of Florida's favorite Governor, when, on "Florida Day," at the Louisville Exposition, several years ago, as he stood up before the eager, anxious thousands who had gathered round him, even amid the fog, clouds, damp and cold of that dreary November day, to hear something of the "Land of Flowers," he wished "for forty acres of Florida climate to spread over the Exposition grounds."

PRODUCTS.

As to our soil, we would have no other if we could; for its many productions, in fruits and vegetables, conclusively prove that our temperatures and upper stratum of earth are in harmony and accord with each other.

Frequently, parties from farther North, when down here, enjoying our genial climate, are struck with what they term "our poor sand," and frequently remark, "Oh, if you just could have our soil down here in this climate, what a country you would have." They lose sight of the fact that the arrangement was made by a Divine hand, and with the same propriety could change the sentence a little, and say, "Oh, if we just had your climate up there, what a country we would have." And so man proposes, but God has disposed of this subject long ago, and we are satisfied. For there is something peculiar in the composition of even "our poor sand." From observation and experience we know that vegetables, of almost any and every variety, can be cultivated and grown to perfection; while oranges, lemons, limes, shaddock, grape fruit and other species of the citrus family, together with guavas, mangoes, pomegranates, bananas, pineapples, alligator pears, sugar apples and many other tropical fruits are in their native element and clime, and produce prolifically. The arrowroot, too, grows in abundance, and if the inhabitants would only turn their attention to its culture, soon its conversion into flour and starch would, beyond all doubt, yield the operators an annual income of several hundreds of thousands of dollars. And then, again, we should deserve reproach were we to omit to say that hemp grows well with us, and its cultivation could be made profitable. Now these statements, the truth of which can be easily ascertained by a visit to these parts, are introduced somewhat in the nature of proof as to the fertility of Hillsborough county sand.

N. DIXON,

TAMPA, FLORIDA.

—— MANUFACTURER OF ——

AND

CYPRESS LUMBER

FLOORING,

DROP SIDING AND CEILING,

Turned and Scroll Work; Pine and Cypress Mouldings; Lath and Shingles.

ORANGE AND VEGETABLE CRATES.

Fancy Pickets a Specialty.

AN AVENUE IN AN ORANGE GROVE.

WATERS.

The principal bodies of water may be summed up in Tampa Bay, Old Tampa Bay, Hillsborough Bay and Hillsborough river.

The industries are as diversified as the character of its inhabitants is varied.

FISH AND OYSTERS.

The waters which we mentioned above and the many beautiful lakes which are dotted all over its surface afford admirable fishing grounds, where the amateur can find sport with his rod, and the regular fisherman fish for the market, and wages for his labor, while in the bays oysters and clams are found in plenty and abundance.

FRUIT.

The fruit grower has no occasion to lament over the profits which he reaps from his groves of oranges and other fruitage, even under the present greedy grab system of the middle-men.

CROPS.

The farmer finds a remunerative employment in tilling a soil which readily brings good crops of sea island cotton, tobacco, sugar cane, rice, potatoes and all truck stuff and which always finds a ready market.

PASTURAGE FOR CATTLE.

It is hardly necessary to say that some portions of our land furnish excellent natural pasturage for cattle, and that so profitable has it proved that there are many in this county whose wealth, acquired solely by raising and shipping cattle, is astonishing.

TURPENTINE.

The "Queen of the Forest," as some one has called our large, tall pine tree, invites the attention of the turpentine farmer, and opens to the saw-mill men employment in which there has already been found, by some in our midst, independence and wealth.

TRUCK GARDENING.

Truck gardening is also extensively engaged in, and during the entire year vegetables of various descriptions and variety constitute in part wholesome food for the tables; and in the early spring time fine large strawberries, whose luscious appearance would bring water to the mouth of the most fastidious epicure, are served at home as ambrosial delicacies, while in large quantities the juicy berries are shipped to the frozen homes of our Northern friends.

PURSUITS.

Of course, as a matter of natural and necessary consequence, we have among us those who follow the ordinary pursuits of life, and do mercantile and other business; some being engaged in the retail, others in the wholesale trade, while frequently the two are combined. But the further consideration of the many and various ways, for only a few have been mentioned, and those in only a cursory manner, in which a livelihood and, quite often, independence can be attained, we must defer for the present, trusting that the patient reader will follow us on to that part of this pamphlet which will treat more in detail the different pursuits and avocations of the inhabitants.

POPULATION.

The population of the county has increased within the last few years in an enormous ratio, the census of 1880 giving us only 5,814 inhabitants, while present calculations give us upwards of 8,721. And as long as the present tide of immigration continues to inundate our every section with respectable and desirable citizens we need have no fears that our fertile and productive soil will remain untilled; that our fish will by their continued reproduction block our streams in their course; that our oyster-bars and clam-beds will remain unnoticed and untouched; that our swamp and overflowed lands will not be drained and converted into rice and sugar plantations; that our pine forests will continue in their primeval wealth and grandeur; that our natural pastures will not be utilized, or that any of the other many natural endowments and facilities will not meet with the high development of which they are susceptible and for which an all-wise Creator designed them. Already many sail and steam vessels, burdened with rich and valuable merchandise, many times more valuable than the fabled "golden fleece," continually glide into our harbors and proudly ride the rolling waves of our lovely waters. Even now, the iron steed, manacled by man to the narrow track leading from the North, comes whistling through our choicest sections, bringing in his train of cars the rich products of the North and West, and many settlers from every portion of the globe, making us cosmopolitan in our citizenship. Owing to a shortness of time, as well as some unfavorable circumstances, we have been unable to ascertain with correctness and exactness the value of the vessels and cargoes which yearly deposit their freights at Tampa and other points along our coast. Yet this much we have observed, that notwithstanding the completion of a railroad to this point, the freights arriving by water have not diminished one iota, but on the contrary have materially increased, as is evidenced by the fact that only a few weeks since the Tampa Steamship Company were necessitated to make additions to their already spacious warehouses. We have also further observed that it was necessary several months ago for the South Florida Railroad Company to increase their freight depot to just double its original capacity.

Such facts as these, the reader will confess, evince progress, enterprise and a glorious future. We must confess that the old fogyism, which has to a great extent existed to the detriment of progress and push in other sections of our State, did for a long time retard the growth of Hillsborough county; but, owing to the overrulings of a Divine Providence, or to the skill of our efficient and far-seeing physicians who practice the Æsculapian art among us, those who were imbued with no ideas of advancement or progress are now enjoying, we hope, sweet rest upon the plains of Elysium, and if not, then Pluto is the one whom we are to commiserate in his continual contentions with their stand-still spirits and Micawber-like enthusiasm. In closing these general remarks, we do not hesitate to say that the mortality of this county will bear us out in stating that almost total freedom from sickness and diseases can and may be enjoyed among us; however, we anticipate, as we design devoting an article to the healthfulness and immunity from diseases in this county.

POST OFFICES IN THE COUNTY.

ALAFIA.
ANONA.
BAY VIEW.
BLOOMINGDALE.
CLEAR WATER HARBOR.
CORK.

DISTON.
DUNEDIN.
JOHN'S PASS.
KEY STONE PARK.
KEYSVILLE.
LIMONA.
YELLOW BLUFF.

MANGO.
PERU.
PINELLAS.
PLANT CITY.
TAMPA.
TARPON SPRINGS.

"H. B. PLANT."

THE LEADING HOTEL OF TAMPA.

Near depot and steamboat wharves and overlooking the River and Bay. First-class in every respect, and ample accommodation for 150 guests. Special attention given to culinary department. After a flourishing season of only four months last winter, 2,967 were entertained, and the house is now closed for extensive repairs. Opens 1st of October; terms $4 a day and upwards, according to location of room. The following notice of the house is from the *Tribune*.

THE H. B. PLANT.—The above-named hotel was opened to the public December 12th, and has instantly established itself as a first-class hostelry in all respects. It is located on the river front, 100 feet from the main depot of the South Florida Railroad, fifty yards from the steamboat landing and one square from the office of the Southern Express Company. The building is a handsome two-story frame, containing forty rooms and covering an area of 8,100 square feet. A striking feature of this hotel is its superior arrangements. The halls and stairways are broad, and so constructed as to give the most excellent ventilation. The rooms are all "front" or "outside" apartments, each with two plate-glass windows, large, fitted with marble-top furniture and the best beds that can be procured. The rooms on the ground floor are all furnished with black walnut. The parlor, office and reading rooms are all specially fine and conveniently arranged. The dining room seats 100 people. The kitchen is a model of perfection, while the ice-house and store-room is all that could be desired. Surrounding the house is 6,000 square feet of piazza. Mr. Anderson will shortly have an artesian well on the grounds, and will spare neither pains nor money to make the H. B. Plant above comparison in Southern Florida. He has been in the hotel business for many years, and is thoroughly versed in efficiently managing a house of this superior character.

SPENCER HENDERSON & CO.,

WHOLESALE DEALERS IN

BUGGIES, ✻ WAGONS,

❊ HARNESS, ETC. ❊

TAMPA, FLORIDA.

HORSES AND MULES

Bought and sold, and for hire.

◁ HAY AND GRAIN FOR SALE. ▷

❊ TEAMS AT ANY AND ALL HOURS. ❊

TERMS EASY.

S. P. Hinckley. H. W. Fuller.

HINCKLEY & FULLER,

ORANGE BUYERS AND PACKERS,

AND WHOLESALE DEALERS IN

GRAIN, HAY, FLOUR, ETC.

—— TAMPA, FLORIDA. ——

FLORIDA ORANGES.

Oranges selected, packed and shipped to order in any amount. We make a specialty of this business and pack nothing but choice fruit. Fruit guaranteed to be perfectly sound and in good keeping condition WHEN SHIPPED.

Terms Cash in advance.

REFERENCE.

Bank of Tampa, or any of the Reliable Merchants or Citizens of Tampa.

Prices quoted and special reference given when required.

Orders respectfully solicited.

Hinckley & Fuller, Tampa, Fla.

N. B.—The Orange Season is from Nov. 1st to May 15th.

TAMPA BAY FROM THE MOUTH OF THE RIVER.

ST. JAMES HOTEL

FRANKLIN STREET,

TAMPA, FLORIDA.

NEWLY FURNISHED.

FIRST CLASS IN ALL ITS APPOINTMENTS.

Has Four Hundred and Fifty Feet of Covered Veranda, with all the comforts of a family home.

Captain Thomas White, late proprietor of the Magnolia House, Darien, Ga., will be pleased to entertain his friends and the traveling public when they visit Tampa.

THOMAS WHITE, MANAGER.

TAKE
THE ✵ KEY ✵ LINE

(Florida Railway and Navigation Co.)
to all Points North or West.

LOW RATES. THROUGH CARS. QUICK TIME.

— THE —
✵ QUICK ✵ THROUGH ✵ ROUTE ✵
— FROM —
SOUTH FLORIDA POINTS,

IS NOW VIA

Orlando, the Tavares, Orlando and Atlantic Railway and the Key Line.

THROUGH SLEEPING CARS ORLANDO TO MONTGOMERY, ALA.

The finest and most economical Summer Resort, **AMELIA BEACH**, Fernandina, Fla., is reached only via this line.

SEND TO ADDRESSES BELOW FOR FULL INFORMATION.

D. E. MAXWELL,   A. O. MacDONELL,
General Superintendent.   Gen. Pass. and Ticket Agt.

FERNANDINA, FLORIDA.

W. G. COLEMAN, Gen. Trav. Agt., Jacksonville, Fla.

TAMPA.

Situated upon the right bank of the Hillsborough river, from which the county takes its name, and at a distance of several hundred yards from its mouth, which opens into Hillsborough Bay, Tampa is, geographically, the most interesting and pleasing feature of the whole county, and, by virtue of its position, is destined within the near future to rival the present metropolis of the State in every respect and particular.

Up to within a very recent period, Tampa, as has been said with truth of all sections of Middle and South Florida, was comparatively little known, on account of her very limited communication with the outside world, notwithstanding the fact that her history dates back to the year 1824, at which time Captain Brooke established a military post for five miles on and around the now existing Federal reservation, known as Fort Brooke, and which, during the old Indian troubles in this State, constituted the principal general hospital for the army. But most of the buildings which then stood upon the reservation have been destroyed either by time or the hand of man, there remaining only two, which serve as monumental memorials to the by-gone days. And with your permission, kind reader, we will here digress somewhat from Tampa proper, and cursorily glance at this lovely spot, which lies adjacent to, and of a right should, and in all probability will be a part of Tampa, for no act of Congress would raise to a greater degree the high appreciation and hearty endorsement of any session than that one which would donate Fort Brooke to Tampa, to be used for a park and other public purposes. We hesitate not to say that in point of picturesqueness and beauty it has not a rival spot even in the poets' loved Italia. In the center, and in fact surrounding and all over this lovely creation of Nature's, there are clumps and clusters of large, grand old live oaks, which are adorned and bedecked by Nature with the festoons of beautiful mosses which hang touching the grassy ground beneath the swinging boughs of the spreading trees. These gray-green living monuments of ages past serve not only as beautiful and natural ornaments to the place, but at the same time afford a cool and refreshing shade to the invalid and tourist, whose ejaculations of surprise, admiration and pleasure evince his gratitude to that star which directed him to these parts and to such a spot. In the spring time and summer months the festive picnicker may be found on almost every day under the shady branches of the beautiful grove.

PALMETTO HOTEL, TAMPA.

PALMETTO HOTEL,

Tampa, Florida.

Just built and newly furnished, is one of the largest, handsomest and most commodious Hotels in South Florida. Three stories high, with a five story observatory. Wide halls and spacious verandas—affording ample promenade space on two sides. One hundred rooms, large and airy, and finished in elegant papers. Furniture and fixtures complete. Bath-rooms and laundry-rooms, etc., attached. The South Florida Railroad has a special platform in front of the Hotel for the accommodation of its guests. One acre in the hotel grounds. Observatory affords a splendid view of the Bay and surrounding country, and opportunity to drink in the sea breeze.

This Hotel can be leased by application to the

Hillsborough County Real Estate Agency,

TAMPA, FLA.

drinking in and enjoying to the full the soft Gulf breezes which come stealing to him through the mossy branches of many a tree.

At present the normal beauty of the place is somewhat marred by the fences which have been erected around and through it by private citizens, one person having attempted to homestead it, and six others having pre-empted it. No satisfactory end can be seen to the contentions of these private parties, and it is the opinion of many of the people that no one individual will get possession of Tampa's natural park, their prayer being a petition to Congress to bestow it where it properly belongs—to the city, *pro bono publico*.

But to return to Tampa, from which we did not intend to stray so long; however, Fort Brooke is naturally a part of Tampa, and is so closely allied and so situated that we may as well consider it technically as a part of Tampa, and so dispose of it now. As we premised above, the military reservation extended in its original for five miles around; but in 1847 Congress donated 160 acres of it to the county as a site for the town, the situation of which 160 acres we have given in our description of the location of Tampa, and from time to time the limits of the original reservation have been narrowed down by placing portions of it on the market until it has reached its present size of 148 acres and over which the fight between several parties is now going on. Without the least fear that the truthfulness of our statement will be called into question, we assert that there is no other city or town in South Florida, aye, or in all Florida, which offers to the tourist and invalid as many and as varied *natural* attractions and advantages as Tampa, the Queen of the Bays. Here, those who come from the chilling blasts and freezing weather of their Northern homes to find in mid-winter a moderate and bracing atmosphere and a salubrious climate, have not only a charming and desirable resort with the qualities they seek, but also free from fogs and rainy days.

CYCLONES.

Another striking and favorable peculiarity of our section is that it is situated in that belt which exempts it from the disastrous cyclones and tornadoes which so often visit other sections both north and south of us. It would be gross injustice to our section, and an unpardonable fault of ours, were we to omit to say that instead of fogs, and damp and chill and rain in winter, our skies are usually bright and clear and blue, and our atmosphere free from over-moisture, while here, as in all South Florida proper, the "rainy season" generally commences along towards the latter part of June or first July, and extends to the middle of August or first September. During this "rainy season," which is not a continual deluge of rain, but more like April weather, giving us an abundance of "sunshine and showers," most of the orange groves are planted, though some practical growers prefer to plant in midwinter, while the sap is down.

But while Tampa holds out such advantages and inducements to the tourist and invalid, it offers equally favorable opportunities to all practical business men and workers who desire a home in this favored spot of the American Italy; for even now, with not a thickly populated tract of country extending all around it for miles, the fall of hammers, the humming of saws, the blasts of whistles, and the hurry and vim of its busy, active citizens, tell plainly of present progress and a fixed determination not to fall short of the greatness which is continually predicted for the place by the thousands who now annually seek its balmy air and genial climate for health or pleasure. It is the county site of the county, and although its incorporation only includes the original grant of 160 acres with a population of from 1,200 to 1,500, yet, within a radius of a mile, the suburbs, all of which are laid off consistent with the streets of the city proper, are so well settled up as to swell the number of inhabitants to 2,500; and at the next municipal election it is proposed to extend the limits of the incorporation so as to include all the suburban portions to which we referred just above.

NATIONALITIES.

It is true of Tampa, as of the county, that the society here is extremely cosmopolitan in its character, almost every State in the Union, and nearly every civilized nation of the world, being fairly represented among us; which fact, we take it, offers special inducements to any who desire to become permanent settlers among us. Here the German can find Germans, the Frenchman French, the Swede those of his native tongue, while the English and Scotch are as numerous as our citizens from our own Northern States.

RELIGIONS OR CHURCHES.

The religious facilities, too, of the place have also peculiar attractions for the stranger, there being a pastor in charge of an organized church of nearly every denomination, and on the Sabbath morn the chimes of many church bells, ringing out from all parts of the city, invite the devout to participate in the services of the day.

SCHOOLS.

In point of schools we have kept pace with the times, there being now one well organized public school and several fine private ones, some of which prepare pupils for the freshman and sophomore classes in our colleges.

TELEPHONE AND TELEGRAPH.

Within the past year the Bell Telephone Company has stretched its wires throughout our streets, and these, with the lines of two telegraph companies, act as obstacles to the flight of the average small boy's kite.

HOTELS.

As to accommodations in hotels and boarding houses, Tampa keeps pace with communities of exceedingly greater and denser population. We must confess, however, that up to within a few years back Tampa was behind in this respect; but at the present writing the H. B. Plant, the St. James, the Palmetto, the Collins House, the Orange Grove and the Craft House offer to the public accommodations well worthy of a larger city. In fact, all of these hotels were so well patronized during the last season, and which is admitted by all to have been one of Florida's poorest, that they found themselves crowded for room, and the H. B. Plant, though a new house, built during the past year, is now closed for extensive additions. Besides these hotels, there are various boarding houses, some of whose appointments and conveniences admit of no superiority in the State. The price of board varies according to the amount of style, etc.; good accommodations, however, can be had for from $4 to $3.50 per day.

SPORTS.

During the winter months Tampa is the headquarters of quite a number of sportsmen, who make either daily or weekly excursions for game or pleasure, down the Bay, up the river or into the interior, and they always report a most successful and enjoyable time. Deer, bears, squirrels, quail, wild ducks and innumerable kinds of sea birds and every kind of fresh and salt water fish are found easily and in abundance. In the summer months, turtling and turtle-egg hunting, as well as graining or gigging the tarpon, jew or other large species of fish, with frequent baths in the

BRANCH'S OPERA HOUSE, TAMPA.

briny waters, give amusement and healthful exercise to the tourist and sportsman.

In mid-winter, the spacious piazzas of our hotels and boarding-houses present a peculiar appearance to the Northern stranger, who, for the first time, strolls down our streets; for while he remembers, with a shiver, that the chilling breezes and bleak hills of the higher latitude, from which he has come, prevent any outdoor exercise but that which is absolutely necessary, he sees crowds of comfortable, cosy-looking loungers, in large easy chairs or comfortable benches, drinking in the balmy air and genial sunshine, while they discuss the pleasures of a semi-tropical resort. And the natives who find time to lounge themselves, are gratified, interested and often amused in watching the movements and actions of the tourists as they saunter down our wide plank walks, stopping here to admire the beauty and elegance of the spreading oak or natural shade; there, to wonder at the freshness and fragrance of the beautiful flower yards; yonder, to guess at the variety of some growing tropical fruit, or halting in astonishment before the show-windows of some taxidermist to gaze with enthusiastic pleasure at the plumage of our beautiful birds or the forms of our peculiar animals, oftentimes going into ecstacies when they have purchased a small "gator" or some other curio to send back to Northern friends.

During "the season," the pleasure-lover and seeker can betake himself to the opera or theatre, where he will be entertained by first-class traveling troupes, or in a more quiet way enjoy himself in the brilliant parlors of the social-loving at a pleasant game of cards or a jolly game of thumbs.

Our spreading oaks with their bending branches, overhanging the steep banks of the picturesque Hillsborough, afford a magnificent shade to the amateur fisherman, as he throws his fishing line into its clear waters and brings into his boat, with pleasing rapidity, the many fine and different species of fish found in these waters. Safe and comfortable row-boats can be easily and readily hired for a small consideration, and nothing is more healthful or delightful than a row upon the river late in the afternoon, when the heat and toil of the day is done; or, better still, in early evening, when "the diadem which crowns the night of our cloudless skies" sheds her soft and delicate light over the silent earth and the rippling waters.

On account of the increased demand for speedy transportation between Tampa and points along the Manatee river, which the completion of the South Florida Railroad has made, an elegant and commodious side-wheel steamer has been put on, and regularly makes the run between Tampa and all the points along the Manatee river. To make it all the more pleasant for any who may come to these hospitable shores, this magnificent floating palace, under the command of one of the most experienced and courteous officers of this coast, makes tri-weekly excursions down the Bay as far as Egmont Key, where it stops long enough to allow the gay passengers a stroll upon the sandy beach to gather the beautiful shells and crystals washed up by the everrolling surf, or a pleasant bath in the briny deep; then proceeding on its return, calls and stops at every place of special interest or attraction along the Manatee.

The other many ways of amusement and pleasant diversion, which lie within the easy reach of every visitor, we cannot stop to enumerate or notice, but sincerely hope that the reader will soon have the pleasure of experiencing them all in person, and of testing the truth of our every statement.

We have already spoken of the city's size and limits; but in this connection we wish to say further that the streets are laid off at right angles running nearly north and south, east and west, and are eighty feet in width, thus giving ample room for shade trees along the sidewalks and in the center of the streets. The blocks are an acre square, and while in the business part of the city the buildings are closely and compactly built together, in those parts where the dwellings are found the blocks are usually divided into only four lots, so that around nearly every private residence

CLARKE & KNIGHT,	S. A. JONES & CO.,
Wholesale and Retail Dealers in	THE * OLD * RELIABLE
HARDWARE, STOVES,	—FOR—
TINWARE. Etc.	**SASH, DOORS, BLINDS,**
	—PAINTS.—
Agents for the HAZARD POWDER CO. Also for the celebrated ACME HARROW, the best known Cultivator for orange trees.	And all kinds of Builders' Supplies.
	Established 1879.

The Hillsborough County Real Estate Agency,
PUBLISHERS OF THIS BOOK.
—SEE SIGN OVER CUT.—
WASHINGTON ST., TAMPA, FLA.

is the large old-fashioned Southern yard in which are planted orange trees or other ornamental evergreens, while a portion of it is devoted to flowers of not only the common and hardier kind, but plants and exotics of the most tender and delicate nature, whose fragrance and perfume and freshness and bloom add so much to the beauty and attractiveness of the place during the whole year.

Some people in the past have been inconsiderate enough to complain of the heavy walking through the sand of our streets, and therefore, recently, the "city fathers" determined to have wide plank walks, made of the best and most durable timber, put down along the line of all the principal streets, and ere this goes to press there will not be a lot in Tampa around which there will not be a new plank walk, so that one can go all over the city and never step in the sand.

The Court House, a large, well-built and well-proportioned two-story frame building, is a creditable "temple of justice," situated in the center of one of the central blocks, and besides containing the court rooms and necessary offices for the county officials, has also a large hall which heretofore has been used as a town hall; but as the city is so rapidly developing, of course the day is not far distant when it will have its own elegant structure. The yard, which is well kept, is enclosed with a nice picket fence, while from its towering cupola may be seen and heard the town clock.

Three weekly newspapers are published here, viz, the *Tribune*, the *Guardian* and the *South Florida Messenger*; the two first are political organs, and the latter one only an instrument to advertise the real estate handled by one of our real estate agencies.

Tampa is quite a business place, there being merchants engaged in all the various branches of merchandise, some doing a general business, while others confine themselves to the wholesale or retail trade in some particular line, and they all seem to do well. This is the most convenient and accessible market for a very large scope of country, so that really its business extends into nearly all of the neighboring counties.

The city proper is situated, as we have before said, on the east side of the river; but within the last few years so rapidly has the western side been settled up that it now goes by the name of West Tampa, and to establish convenient communication between this suburb and the city proper a ferry boat is run back and forth continually during the day; but we have good reasons for believing that soon this will be done away with, and that in less than a year's time a bridge will span the river, connecting more closely the two places. Leading out from the northern part of the city are three avenues about a quarter of a mile apart and running parallel with each other for more than five miles, and from the limits of the city to their ends are scattered all along these avenues flourishing orange groves, generally of five or ten acres in size, and upon which nice cosy-looking cottages have been erected by their respective owners. There are also several smaller and less important avenues leading out from the eastern side, and all of these, both great and small, have been called after some Northern or Western State. Tampa's prospective railroad connections are more than ordinarily good, there being a number of railroads now building which by their charters are compelled to come to Tampa, and if only one-half of the prospective roads ever reach us there will be no place in all Florida, or perhaps in the South, which will be so favored with railroad facilities. From its geographical position and water communication, Tampa must and will be the distributing point for the trade from the North and Northwest for South Florida, and the key to the commerce of the West Indies and Central and South America. Already we have one railroad—the South Florida—completed and nicely equipped, and which runs daily trains from this point to Sanford on the St. Johns river, giving a pleasant ride of five hours and a half from the grand old river to the glorious old Bay, so that passengers leaving Jacksonville on the mail boat at 2:30 P. M. one day arrive in Tampa at 2:30 the next day; fare, $11.75.

As yet her population has not warranted gas works, but the town is well lighted with street lamps, which give the place quite a citified air at night.

The Masons have a lodge building, in the hall of which they and the Odd Fellows hold regular meetings, while other societies formed for culture and sociability hold forth in other quarters of the city. Her Base Ball Club continues to retain the belt over all other clubs of South Florida, while the Tampa Guards enable her to boast of the average militia organization. And now, in concluding this imperfect sketch of the county site and its attractions, we can conceive of nothing more appropriate than to say "the half has never been told." After all we have said as to her many attractions and her desirableness as a place of resort or permanent settlement, we promise, in all the sincerity of our hearts, that you will never regret it if you come among us, either as a visitor or a settler. Some one said of Italy's famous city, "See Venice and die." We say, "See Tampa and *live*."

RESIDENCE AND ORANGE GROVE.

OTHER PLACES.

While the many other attractive and desirable towns which adorn this county with their enterprise and facilities, and beautify it with their architectural edifices and buildings, are by far inferior to Tampa in point of size and population, yet none will admit of any superiority in prosperity and glorious prospects for the future; for this whole county is enjoying a "boom," which will not suffer one section to remain far in the rear of the others, and it is a boom, too, which will continue as long as the sweet winding waters of the Hillsborough wend their way to the ocean stream, singing merrily of the balmy air and the sunny skies which reflect the brilliant rays of a semi-tropical sun upon their dancing waves. Among the most important of these is

PLANT CITY,

named in honor of H. B. Plant, the principal factor in the Plant Investment Company, which controls such an overwhelming interest in the railroads of Florida. It is situated twenty-three miles east of Tampa on the South Florida Railroad, and within a little over a year's time has increased in population from several scattered families to fifteen hundred bona fide inhabitants. Such an enormous and miraculous increase is due to the scope of country surrounding it, and also to the push and energy of those who had invested in lands at and around that point previous to the completion of the road. For its age, we cavil not to say that it is the largest and most thriving little city in the South. It has recently been incorporated, and its orderly yet busy and active citizens declare that its present prosperity shall ever continue, and that its rapid growth is not of the mushroom character. Its accommodations in hotels and boarding houses are pronounced good by all those who have visited it, either in search of a home or in the pursuit of health or pleasure. There are, as any one would naturally suppose, a number of stores, doing all the different branches and twigs of merchandise, and all the other many avocations of life have their quota of representatives.

PINELLAS

we will next consider, which, on account of its other many natural facilities besides its accessibility to the health-restoring breezes of the Bay and Gulf, is the proposed site of a sanitary city to be constructed after the suggestion of Dr. Richardson, of London, a movement which is attracting the attention of the whole world, and one in which all the civilized nations of the world are expected to enter. The fact that

Drs. Toner, of Washington, Chadwick, of Boston, Wilson, of Philadelphia, headed by Van Bibber, of Baltimore, all eminent physicians, visited this section for purposes of investigation, and the still further fact that their reports were most complimentary and flattering, is sufficient evidence that this design, which has already enlisted the sympathies and well wishes of every thinking man, will be crowned with success. Aught else that we could say of Pinellas would sound of mockery, so we will now view

DUNEDIN,

as she is situated upon the coast of the Gulf. The settlements in and around this place are quite numerous, there being, too, some of the finest orange groves in the State all through that region. The character of the land is the first-rate pine which we describe in our article on the soil, and several saw-mills have been erected to utilize the magnificent timber to be found on all such.

ALAFIA

is situated on the river which bears the same name, and that section of country embraces Peru and many other small towns. The indispensable pursuits of life are of course prosecuted there; but that feature which attracts more attention than all others is its abundance of hammock and swamp lands, upon which are cultivated the vegetables of every variety. Though at the present time it is lacking in railroad facilities, the river affords a fair transportation, which has for many years been taken advantage of. We might, were we not tenacious of time, go on to enumerate and partly describe the many advantages and opportunities of ANONA, BAY VIEW, BLOOMINGDALE, MANGO, KEYSVILLE, and so on; but we will draw these sectional remarks to a close by noticing in an extremely cursory manner,

THONOTOSASSA LAKE,

which for beauty and grandeur has not a rival sheet of water this side of Niagara Falls. At the time of writing it is at its lowest, but now measures two miles in length and one in width. Upon the beach of this small inland sea are situated beautiful cottages, encircled with the native oak and the evergreen orange. It teems with the most delicious quality of trout and other fish, and it is quite notorious that this lake affords one of the best fresh-water fisheries in South Florida. "It is the pride of the citizens of the community, ... who feast upon the beauty of its waves and breathe the purity and vigor of its breezes."

THE SOIL.

If one should travel through this county at a reasonable rate, noticing casually its white-sandy appearance, and having his eyes blind to its varied vegetation, no conclusion would be more plausible and probable to him than that one which would declare the productive lands to be of a very small per cent. Its exceeding diversity and varied character might in all probability escape his observation, and consequently the fact that it is susceptible of the cultivation of crops not only not grown in the states generally, but also of those things which characterize the tropical climes. If one would avoid a mistake as to the character of the soil, its white-sandy appearance must not in any instance be taken as evidence against it, for there is certainly, as we have said before, something peculiar in the composition of this sand which peculiarly adapts it to the growth of the fruits and plants of this climate, and frequently a more close and thorough examination will bring to light the fact that a goodly per cent. of it is composed of the debris of shells and carbonate of lime. And potash, which is found in the palmetto flats, and which is generally pronounced the poorest land, is a constituent element of plant food, and evinces the fact that in the presence of alkaline salt nature provides what is lacking in the soil. On account of its diversity and varied character the soil is commonly classed as first, second and third-rate pine lands, and as high and low hammock, and swamp lands. The pine lands, as is observed by all, constitute much the larger portion of the country, and all the classes can be utilized in one way or another. The poorest soil, even, in the third-class pine lands is not worthless, for upon it can be found the most desirable pasturage for cattle; and the palmetto, which generally grows in such an abundance upon it, is now being converted into the best and finest wrapping paper, while its choicest leaves are made into fans.

In regard to the first-class pine land, we quote from J. S. Adams, ex-Commissioner of Immigration, who published a pamphlet in 1869: " It has nothing analogous to it in any of the other states. Its surface is covered for several inches with a dark vegetable mould, beneath which, to the depth of several feet, is a chocolate sand loam, mixed, for the most part, with limestone pebbles, resting on a substratum of marl, clay or limestone rock. The fertility and durability of this description of land may be estimated from the well-known fact that it has, on the upper Suwannee and several other districts, yielded during fourteen years of successive cultivation, without the aid of manure, four hundred pounds of sea island cotton to the acre, and the lands are as productive as ever, so that the limit of their durability is still unknown." The second-class pine lands are the most numerous, and are found from experience to be quite productive, and from their fertility and healthfulness they are preferred to the richer hammock lands, which are more or less sickly. This class is the kind of land upon which are found most of our beautiful bearing groves. The high hammock lands are not, as is often erroneously supposed, either very damp or subject to overflow during the greater part of the year; but, on the contrary, do not require either any drainage or ditching or levees. They are spots interspersed here and there throughout our pine lands, and as the same Mr. Adams suggests, can be easily cultivated, while the cultivator can reside upon the healthy pine lands, provided his residence upon the hammock land should be found to produce sickness. The low hammock lands are generally wet, and as a consequence have to be drained before they are fit for cultivation, and from experience it has been proved that this class affords the best soil for the cultivation of rice and sugar cane, neither of these crops being injured by great moisture. The swamp lands are considered the richest and most desirable, and it is mainly upon these lands that our early vegetables, which are shipped to the North, are grown. Sugar cane also does exceedingly well upon it, and in some instances as much as four hogsheads of sugar have been made from the cane produced upon an acre, and fair and reasonable estimates show that these lands of Florida will produce sufficient sugar to supply the present demand of the whole United States. But we must return for a few moments to the pine lands, of the abundance and quality of which we have already spoken, as we failed to notice the timber interest. The pines, which grow upon the first and second-class lands to be very large and tall, supply the many saw-mills with most admirable timber, from which is sawed the most durable lumber. And, by way of digression, we may here remark that the lumber business is carried on very extensively in this county, many of the mills taking advantage of the convenient location of the Hillsborough river and other streams to raft their saw logs to the mill and their lumber to market. In the third-class lands, while the trees do not by any means grow to any great height, nor are so well adapted for lumber making, yet they are quite valuable, as they are sufficiently large in circumference to contain an abundance of sap, which gives us crude turpentine from which is made the spirits of turpentine and rosin, two articles of commerce which are daily enhancing in value, as the demand is broadening and increasing, while the supply from the old sources is rapidly declining.

From the many facts we have already stated, we hardly think it worth while to particularly enumerate the many different varieties and kinds of crops and vegetables which may be grown in this county, for from its varied character and conditions you must be satisfied that with proper care and attention anything and everything nearly can be successfully raised.

In reference to the advantages and favoring peculiarities to farming here, we can do no better than to quote the following, which we extract from the *Florida Gazetteer:* "One striking peculiarity of the Florida soil is its easier culture than the stiffer soils. Another is that most of the farm labor and tillage can be performed in those months of the year when the ground is frozen further north. Still another peculiarity is that the fertilizers are applied with a better effect, both because the applications are not carried away by the rains as frequently as they are in higher regions, and because the more porous soil lets in the atmosphere more readily to aid the fertilizer in the work of decomposing the minerals of the soil, and setting free the food elements they contain for the use of the crops grown.

FRUIT GROWING.

The tropical and semi-tropical fruits which are grown in this county are of such great variety, and include so many different kinds, that we are pardonable if we omit to mention quite a number, and furthermore, if we only mention some which justly merit elaboration. Orange culture will of course be the principal object of this chapter, if we may call it such, while the other fruits will be considered in a cursory manner. In taking up each genus of fruit, we do so as they come to our minds, and without any reference either to their natural or logical order.

The PINEAPPLE, which is to a great extent an air plant, is very profitably and easily grown in every section of the county, the climate being very suitable for its production, and the plant depending very little upon the nutrition of the soil. In many of the yards of the private residences in Tampa these plants can be seen in numerous small patches in every stage, from the time of suckering to full bearing. We do not hesitate to say that as soon as we have more thorough and speedy means of transportation for the delicate fruits, this one, which is so juicy and delicious, will be quite an item in the lists of shipments to the Northern markets.

The GUAVA, a tree which is so numerous and so prodigal in its growth and bearing that it almost impresses upon the mind the belief in spontaneous generation, gives us an abundance of its elegant fruit. While its shape and manner of growth resembles the peach more than anything else with which perhaps the reader is familiar, its fruit, in size and general appearance, is more similar to the pear. As yet experiment has devised no other way of utilizing the guava than converting it into jelly and marmalade and preserves; and so superb are the three considered, by even the finest epicures, that if carried on to any considerable extent it would prove one of the best paying industries of Florida. Of course it is understood that the guava is considered one of the most desirable and palatable fruits we have when fresh from the tree.

The MANGO is simply superb; nothing can excel it, and but few fruits can compare with its deliciousness. So far but little attention has been given to its culture, as its fruit is too delicate to bear shipment by the slow transportation we have had, and it was considered too great a delicacy for those who had to look close after those things necessary to secure "meat and bread." There is only one objection to the mango, if objection it be, and that is it is one of those things which you cannot eat gracefully. It has a skin like the apple, and is about the color inside and out of a well-ripened banana, with a seed like an almond, except about four times as large, and is shaped like—a mango. One gentleman living near Tampa planted two mango switches in his yard about eight years ago. Now they are luxuriant trees of about forty feet in height, and he says the crop from one of them this year will bring here, in Tampa, $240.

The SUGAR APPLE, which is a shrub in growth, thrives well as far north as Tampa, and is especially peculiar, as its name indicates, from its extreme sweetness, which renders a taste for it, as well as for many other of the tropical fruits, more or less acquired.

The FIG is readily grown from cuttings, and so vigorous and rapid is its growth that it frequently comes into bearing in two years from planting. The fruit, as all know, is so palatable and healthy, and the cultivation of it so easy, and its preparation for market so simple and inexpensive, that no doubt it will soon command special attention.

The BANANA is one of the most popular and prosperous fruits grown in our section, and is propagated from suckers planted in rich, moist soil. There are quite a number of different varieties, which vary in size as well as in flavor, and all will agree with us in saying that few fruits equal a well-ripened banana in delicacy and flavor.

PLUMS of nearly every description are found growing wild in every section of the county, and from these are made some of the finest and most marketable jellies.

In a few of the yards in Tampa the COFFEE PLANT is successfully grown, and its easy cultivation will warrant its becoming, in time, one of the leading industries of this and other Southern counties. In the sister county below, the first pound of coffee produced in the State was grown last year, and the fact of the grower receiving a premium from the Agricultural Department is evidence of its excellent quality.

Luxuriant GRAPE arbors, giving fruit of endless varieties, flourish throughout the county, and in point of fact they grow wild in the hammock and swamp lands, frequently beautifully and gracefully festooning the trees with their climbing vines. The Scuppernong is the general favorite with us, and is a success beyond all doubt.

The ALLIGATOR PEAR tree (from whence or why it gets its name no one can tell) is a beautiful ornamental shade and fruit tree, much taller than the orange, but of less denseness, both in the branches and foliage, resembling in its growth and appearance the magnolia. The fruit when matured is not very unlike the pear in color and shape, while its size is perhaps two or three times that of an ordinary-sized pear. It has a flavor which is peculiarly its own, and cannot be likened to anything we have ever tasted, and as a relish it is much liked by almost every one who tries it. This fruit suffers no more from transportation than the orange, and as soon as it receives the deserved attention its cultivation will be increased and the Northern markets supplied.

The PEACH, which is grown more or less in all the Southern States, but which is not indigenous to this State, does well with us, in a measure. That is to say, the great difficulty which seems attached to its cultivation with us is our mild winters, which cause irregularity in its fruiting, frequently blooming so early and so often as to cause the tree to drop every bloom for two or three consecutive years.

But the most prominent, important and widely cultivated of all the fruits that are properly and easily produced in this county, as well as in the State, is the ORANGE, with its sister fruits of the citrus family. And under the citrus genus is compassed all the varieties of the orange, lemon, limes, citron, shaddock and grape fruit, numbering in all more than one hundred species. In respect to the cultivation of the orange, Florida, on account of her peculiarities of climate, soil and season, stands superior to all other sections of the globe and will ever maintain her present superiority. But it is only within the last few years that orange growing has assumed the proportions of an industry, although it is more than probable that the Spaniards upon their first settlement of St. Augustine planted and successfully cultivated this now popular fruit. True, that in ante-bellum days, many Floridians planted groves near St. Augustine and along the St. Johns and Indian rivers, and even some on Tampa Bay; but these were more in the nature of ornaments and embellishments of the houses of the independent and rich. Go back twenty years, and you will find that the large proportion of people in South and Middle Florida were too poor to give any attention to orange culture. The struggle was a daily and continuous one for the necessaries of life and no time was left for anything else, and then, too, there were no means of transportation; so that really it was not until after the late war was over, and our State became renowned for its salubrious climate and was flooded with our Northern friends in pursuit of health and pleasure, that the delicious delicacy of the "rich golden fruit," hanging amid the dark green foliage of its mother tree, attracted the eye and awakened a craving for it, which soon increased the demand and thereby started what has since been appropriately termed the "orange fever." And since then down to the present time thousands upon thousands of tourists, invalids and speculators, drawn thither by the reports of the happier forerunners, have continued to come, and hundreds of them, enticed by the promising profitable investment, have purchased lands and planted groves, until now the State is dotted from Jacksonville to Punta Rassa and from the Atlantic to the Gulf with orange groves of every age and size, from the seedlings fresh from the nursery to the full-bearing trees.

On account of the immense number engaged in this industry, it is sometimes asked by unthinking men if the market will not be over-stocked when all these groves come into bearing, and as a necessary sequence the profits become a "minus quantity." The question on its face is absurd, and is almost as foolish as that one which queries, "Will not the boom fall out of South Florida after a while?" To the first question, as to the market becoming over-stocked, a thinking mind will reason, the demand creates a market, the supply controls the price. Where the supply is small the price is high and the demand is limited. Where the supply is great the price becomes low and the demand more general. To bring all the groves in Florida now into bearing simply means to open a larger market for oranges, and to place within the reach of those too poor to buy now this delicious fruit of the South. The prices of oranges may go down, and of a right ought to when the crop is increased, but if a man can get a cent apiece for his crop he can coin money out of a five-acre bearing grove. Moreover, further than this practical way of looking at this question, it is estimated that of the consumption of oranges in the United States only one-twelfth is furnished by Florida, the remaining eleven-twelfths being received from abroad. And right on the face of this it is admitted by all fair judges that of all the oranges in the markets the Florida orange is by far the most superior, which fact is illustrated practically by the ever-recurring fraud of palming off foreign oranges as the fruit from Florida.

As to the second idle question, "Won't the boom fall out of South Florida?" Yes, we answer, that is, when they will have no cold, ice and snow in the North, when "angel health sits ever on their breezes," and they have no pulmonary diseases; when Tampa Bay freezes over, and the orange trees of South Florida are laden with icicles and snow-flakes; when you bankrupt the North, and destroy the balmy air and genial climate of South Florida—then, and not till then, will the boom fall out.

But to return to the orange culture. We might here in this connection enter into an analysis of the climatic influences and the soil to show why the orange is more successfully grown here than in other counties; but when a fact has been generally admitted, we consider that time would be wasted in advancing other proofs. Already at the very lowest calculation there is now invested in orange groves throughout the State more than $10,000,000, with a large and inviting field for much larger investments. This, as well as other Southern counties, did not at first take the "fever" and give much attention to the culture of the orange, owing to the very poor and imperfect modes of transportation for the fruit to market. But now that we are at the terminal point of many railroads projected, and one already completed, this county will not long remain second to any in the State. The soil in nearly every section of the county is adapted to the successful cultivation of the citrus fruits; and where the lands are classed poor, nature has provided an abundance of good and cheap fertilizer which can be readily and cheaply applied in such a manner as to render them very productive. The soil, as has been already remarked, is peculiarly fitted for the application of such fertilizers, and some of our finest groves are on our poorest pine lands. In this connection we quote from Capt. R. W. Shupeldt's (U. S. Navy) Report of Exploration and Surveys: "The soil in which these fine Chimalapa oranges grow is peculiar, being a very clean white sand, . . . and it is on account of this peculiarity of the soil, no doubt, that the fruit is so unusually fine." As to the profits which have been received from such investments, we can only say that time and again a thousand dollars have been cleared from a single acre, and there is one tree twenty-three miles east of Tampa which in 1880 yielded a few over 10,000 oranges. Yet with this, as with all other businesses, there are some few obstacles in the way of certain success. Being a very recent business pursuit, much has yet to be learned by experience and experiments, so that many of the theories in regard to the best modes of cultivation are somewhat conflicting.

In 1880 the number of bearing orange trees in this county was estimated at 18,683, and their yield at 4,409,150, and their value at $45,410.25. Of course with the four years' "boom" the number has enormously increased, and their yield and value correspondingly. We do not think we would be far from right if we were to say that the number, etc., is now double what it was in 1880. The other members of the citrus family, with their numerous different varieties, are also extensively and successfully cultivated throughout the county, although our space forbids an extended notice of them. Below we give an approximate estimate of the cost to bring a piece of wild land into a bearing grove. The price of the land will vary according to location, character, etc. Our calculation is based on a ten-acre tract:

10 acres, say at $1.25, Government price	$12 50
(Private lands run all the way from this to $100 per acre.)	
Clearing and fencing with rails, at $20 per acre	200 00
(This of course depends largely upon the character and location of the land, as well as the accessibility of rail-timber.)	
Dwelling and houses (the dwelling, a cottage of 4 rooms, and plain, rough outhouses)	250 00
1,000 one-year-old trees	75 00
Labor setting out trees	10 00
Expense of cultivating and fertilizing same for eight years, at $75 per year	600 00
	$1,147 50

This is on the assumption that the proprietor does no labor himself and buys his fertilizers. Many ten-acre groves in this county now worth many thousands of dollars were made with far less expense than what this estimate shows. We have in our mind's eye one grove in this county that cannot be bought for $20,000 to-day, that really cost the owner nothing except the original price of the land and his own labor.

And now, in conclusion, we say for further information concerning orange culture we cordially invite you to come to our county and be an eye witness to the means and processes used in it, as the limits of this publication forbid greater elaboration

RAILROADS.

The railroad facilities of this section are as yet comparatively little developed, there now being but one road which traverses this county, and which has its terminus at Tampa. This road furnishes good transportation and accommodations, and the many passengers who continually fill its coaches attest its convenience. It is known as the South Florida Railroad, and connects the St. Johns river on the east with Tampa bay on the west, making the distance of 115 miles in five and a half hours, including stops at the many thriving little villages and towns which have sprung up all along its line. Besides this road eight others have been chartered, and most of which number propose to have their terminus at the head of Tampa Bay, with branches running to various points in the lower counties. Prominent among these proposed roads is the International Railroad and Steamship Line, and very recently Gen. John B. Gordon, its renowned President, remarked while stopping at the H. B. Plant Hotel that in less time than a year he would return to this place on through cars from the North. The Yulee system, or what is now known as the Florida Railway and Navigation Company, already has trains running to within forty miles of our county line, and is making rapid strides towards Tampa, while the Florida Southern and the Jacksonville, Tampa and Key West have a large number of hands grading their road-beds to our desirable city. Of course we do not pretend to say that out of the eight proposed roads none will fall through, although we have no right to question either the good faith or ability of any of them, and we do believe in the sincerity of our hearts, and not without good show of reason, that the larger per cent. will be constructed, not including the International and Yulee systems, which are certain and fixed.

The day is not far distant in the dim future when Tampa, as quite a railroad termini and center, as well as the entry port for the many large vessels sailing between this and the countries of Central and South America, will have assumed the proportions of a city which will surpass anything in the State of Florida, and will place her in the rank to which her position as the Queen of the Bays so justly entitles her.

APPLY TO THIS AGENCY FOR ANYTHING REFERRING TO LAND OR INVESTMENTS.

—READ—

The Advertisement of the

☙HILLSBOROUGH COUNTY❧

REAL ✻ ESTATE ✻ AGENCY

——ON PAGE 70.——

✻ CITY ✻ HOTEL, ✻

TAMPA, FLA.

J. FORQUER & SON, PROPRIETORS.

The City Hotel is situated near the South Florida Railroad depot and convenient to the different wharves. It is entirely new and equipped second to none in Tampa; has forty well-ventilated rooms, each room having an outside window, and rooms of all sizes, single, double and for families. Three stories with halls each way; also open and closed piazzas; and will be ready to open October 1st, with all the modern improvements. With two dining rooms on the European Plan.

TERMS—$2 PER DAY; $10 PER WEEK; $35 PER MONTH.

✺ BAGGAGE ✺ HANDLED ✺ FREE ✺ TO ✺ AND ✺ FROM ✺ HOTEL ✺

Write to this Agency for information on the best and cheapest route to this part of Florida. You can save money by it.

FISH.

The artificial propagation and raising of fish has within recent years attracted much attention and caused many experimental tests to be made both in America and Europe; but with us in Hillsborough county, who possess such an extensive coast line, and whose large bays and many lakes afford such admirable fishing grounds, this question has no practical interest. The great abundance and variety of fish to be found in our bays, rivers, creeks and lakes, make fish ponds of an artificial nature quite unnecessary. All our waters abound in fish of the most excellent quality, such as the black bass, pike, jack, trout, bream, and the many varieties of the perch family, among which may be classed the red snapper, grouper, sheepshead, red fish, black fish, pompano, Spanish mackerel, rock fish, mullet, and a long list of what are called "pan fish." As an economical and delicious article of food, fish is appreciated and used throughout the length and breadth of the universe, so it is no surprising fact that catching and selling them constitutes an industry from which no inconsiderable revenue is derived. Along the coast of Hillsborough and at many points in the bays fishing is engaged in very extensively, and besides the immense quantities which are consumed at home, numbers are packed in ice and shipped fresh to other states, while large quantities are cleansed, salted, dried and sent to the interior, where the fish are not so abundant. The fishing as a business is done chiefly with seines and nets, and the "strikes," as they call the catch, are frequently astounding to an inland stranger, often running up to hundreds of barrels. Frequent pleasure or sporting excursions are made down the bay to the principal fisheries, and sometimes parties with their families spend several weeks in the enjoyment of this nomadic life and fascinating sport. The "run" of the fish, as the season for fishing is called, begins about the first of October and lasts until sometime late in the spring, during which time many small boats containing parties of two or three can be seen anchored all along the bay and river. Under this head we may also mention the green turtle, which is a staple commodity of these waters. They sell readily here in our markets, and large numbers of them are shipped North alive, where the fastidious taste of epicures makes the demand great and the remuneration for catching and handling considerable.

Oysters and clams are to be found in great abundance all along the coast and at many places in the bays, and are very large and fine indeed. These are only to be found in salt waters, and are taken by means of iron tongs fastened to long wooden handles, and on short notice the oystermen furnish them, to places in the interior, fresh from the beds. In this county all kind of fishing is yet in its infancy, but no doubt as the county becomes more thickly populated, a business of great importance and magnitude will spring out of the fishing interest. In this connection we may throw in a few words in reference to the shell mounds of the State, the largest of which is perhaps found on the old military reservation of Fort Brooke, adjoining Tampa, and which, on account of its size, speaks eloquently of the palatableness of the shell fish as food for the Indians. The archæologists have examined these mounds with much care and interest, and the theory generally arrived at is that once every year or season the Indians, either as a tribe or family, came down to some convenient point on the coast to have a picnic on shell fish, and coming frequently to the same place, and dropping the shells where the fish were eaten, unconsciously and without design on their part these mounds grew to the proportions we now find. Perhaps this is the most rational, common-sense view of accounting for the shell mounds which everywhere bedot the coast of Florida.

A FLORIDA LAKE.

TIMBER INTERESTS.

Strange, indeed, would it be did not this county, whose fine timber, both of pine and cypress is so plentiful and abundant, engage to a considerable extent in the lumber trade, in which, as we have before remarked, there has been found independence and wealth. With a land surface of about 542,928 acres (rough estimate), which is continually being cleared of its timber for purposes of agriculture and improvements in many other ways, our saw-mills are constantly supplied with the most desirable material, the sale of which, after it has undergone the process of sawing and general dressing, is accomplished without any effort whatever on the part of the seller. Until recently, on account of our limited and poor communication with the outside world, the immigration to this section was not nearly so great nor were improvements so general, and as a consequence no small per cent. of the timber which was cut by the natives in the clearing of land for agricultural and horticultural purposes was not utilized, but was on the contrary suffered to remain in heaps of logs, which of course would in a reasonable time decay. Only that portion of it was used which the then limited home consumption demanded; and now, when our facilities for transportation are improving and broadening both in respect to quantity and time, our people would indeed be dead to the times and their interest did they not follow the example of Pensacola and other ports along the Florida coast and establish lumber yards for the shipment of lumber to all parts of our great country. But the excuse which they now have for not so doing, and it is a most legitimate one, is that this section, on account of the immense number of buildings which have been, are being and will be erected, demands more than can be supplied. We clearly see, however, that not far in the future a foreign lumber yard will be established in this county, which, on account of its advantages in the way of water communication, will be one of the best patronized of any in the State, there being but two harbors on the Florida coast which carry on any extensive trade in this line of commerce, and over either of which Tampa Bay can boast—over one because of its not so convenient accessibility to timber, and over the other because of its greater distance by several hundred miles from those points on the Atlantic coast where are found the great lumber markets of the North and East. As we have already endeavored to impress on you, Tampa is quite a commercial center, around which in the radius of many miles there is an extensive scope of country depending upon her for supplies; and since it has been found, by those who have experimented sufficiently to judge, that goods of an imperishable nature can be brought to this point by water with less cost than by rail, we can see no good reason why a foreign lumber yard cannot be established, and instead of allowing the vessels which bring such goods here to return to the Northern ports empty, fill their holds with our sawed yellow pine, which, on account of its quality, and also the sparseness of good building material in other regions, will always enjoy a ready and quick sale in the Northern ports. Both Mexico and Central America depend upon Florida for the cross-ties to be used on their railroads, and points on Tampa Bay are certainly as convenient for their shipment, and in some respects more so, than any of the other harbors; so notwithstanding the insufficient appropriations of Congress up to date, we predict that Tampa within a comparatively short space of time will be the center of a very considerable lumber trade with foreign places, and by foreign we mean such as are not within the limits of the State of Florida, for already from some stations on the South Florida Railroad, and points on the Bay and Manatee river, orders are continually received for fine building material from the mills in this vicinity. As to the quality of Florida timber in general, we can do no better than to make use of a quotation from the New York *Mercantile Journal*, which is also to be found in ex-Commissioner Adams' pamphlet of 1873:

"Yellow pine flooring and step planks from Florida are in fair demand at $30 per thousand feet, while inferior lumber made in North and South Carolina moves slowly at from $23 to $25 per thousand. The yellow pine, so-called, growing in the Carolinas, is objectionable for many reasons. In the first place, the tree is of a different and less enduring species, and has a greater proportion of sap wood and black knots; and in the second place, it is from those trees from which the manufacturers of turpentine and pitch get their material, thus depriving them of the ingredient upon which the durability and peculiar excellence of this kind of wood depends. Owners should always require in their specifications that the yellow pine to be used in first-class buildings should be of the growth of Florida." So we can clearly perceive that which explicates the peculiar and constant demand for the Florida pine is its excellent quality. As to the extent and vastness of the growth of the pine in this and other sections of the State, some idea may be gathered from General Andrew Jackson's celebrated observation, "that the forests were so overgrown with trees of large spreading branches, it was with difficulty that a man even on foot was able to travel through them." Estimating that on a general average each acre of land now contains 5,000 feet of timber, which, however, is an exceedingly low calculation, this county would have in its limits 126,204,000 feet of available lumber, and as the pine is ordinarily generative, the supply of timber in this county, according to the rate of its present consumption, is, we may say, almost inexhaustible, especially as it is positively asserted by parties competent to judge that in the country adjoining Pensacola, notwithstanding her immense mill capacity, the timber grows faster than it can be cut down.

The Bay, the Hillsborough and Alafia rivers, as well as the many smaller streams, afford ample water for the drifting of the many rafts of logs which are continually floated to the mills. The trees having been cut down and cut into convenient lengths, are hauled by the large log-carts to the nearest stream and there connected together into a raft, which, as soon as the tides are favorable, is allowed to drift to the mill, where long ago they have been bargained for. But the pine, we wish you to understand, is not the only tree used in our lumber-making and lumber commerce. Our swamps contain large bodies of the finest cypress, from which can be sawed the most desirable shingles; it is also well adapted to nearly all the purposes for which pine is used, besides it is considerably used in boat and ship-building, and the transportation and sale of this wood to the North and East will in the course of time form no insignificant branch of business.

A FLORIDA RIVER AND HAMMOCK SCENE.

Cedar is also found in large quantities in our swamps and low hammock lands, and it is principally from the Florida mills that all the Northern factories are supplied with their wood material for making pencils and various other articles, and notable among these are Faber's and Dixon's factories. Upon our high hammock lands the live oak, so durable and lasting, is also of very considerable growth, and it is from this tree, which is frequently enormous in size, that most of the ship knees are made, it being the most suitable wood for this and other purposes in ship-building. There are now in this county, by actual count, over thirty mills, some of them not only doing the usual common mill work, but in addition to sawing and general dressing of lumber, some convert it into doors, sashes, blinds and window-sills of various kinds and designs.

Black walnut is also grown in this section, though to a limited extent, but since the cheapness and fertility of the lands will admit of it, and as it is a most vigorous grower, it is proposed to plant a forest of this timber, and from the experimental tests already made nothing short of success is predicted and expected. All along the banks of the streams both large and small, and along the coast, the large and elegant magnolia, with its beautiful and fragrant flowers, is found in its native soil, and also in many places the red bay, which, however, is only a different species of the same family. From these trees is obtained a most desirable wood for cabinet work, on account of its dark color and beautiful veins. It is commonly known as the "Florida mahogany," and as it is of considerable worth and grown without any culture whatever, it will command careful attention and consideration. We are not disposed to praise the Florida pine and other timbers beyond their true worth and just merit, yet we would impress upon those who have been so patient as to read the simply stated and unvarnished facts, not to let Florida be undervalued and misunderstood in this respect, since timber constitutes one of the important industries of the world. And since in our county grow well nearly all the various kinds of woods—woods from which we can make houses, ships, furniture, barrel-staves and hoops, in fact, articles of nearly any and every description—we would indeed be blind to our own interests, as we remarked in the beginning, did we not vigorously grasp the many natural advantages and not allow them to pass untouched and unnoticed.

CATTLE INTERESTS

No other industry in South Florida up to within a few years past was engaged in near so extensively or by any means embraced so much capital as that which is commonly known as stock-growing, the principal and chief branch of which pursued in this county being the raising of cattle of the more important stamp. Until quite recently more wealth and riches have accrued to the dealer through this investment than any other, a fact which conspicuously explains the number of shrewd men connected with it. Even the tillage of the soil was a secondary matter. And at present, as in the past, in all parts of the county are to be found numerous herds of larger or smaller cattle. They are permitted by their owners to run at-large through the woods, and they thrive and prosper in a manner remarkably well and entirely satisfactory to the parties interested. Mr. F. A. Hendry, a large cattle owner, in an article published in the *Semi-Tropical Journal*, says: "Hillsborough is a beautiful county, and regarded as very pleasant and healthy, and formerly a large stock-raising district, but as the country becomes settled, farming and fruit-growing have to a considerable extent taken the place of cattle-raising, though the county is still sparsely settled and feeds about 50,000 head of cattle, and is regarded as a fair cattle range." The expenses involved in raising cattle are extremely small, there being none whatever connected with the pasturage, and it is only twice during the whole year that they "round up," mark and brand the new calves, giving little or no other attention other than this. In fact, so little expense attends this investment that the hide and tallow of a four-year-old steer will return a surprising profit upon the cost of his keep. The character of the cattle raised in this county is very different from the Texas cattle; ours presents a small appearance, with thick, heavy necks and fore parts, while the loins are contracted, and at the age of three years will generally clear 300 or 400 pounds. The beef is sold readily at from six to ten cents per pound, the price varying according to the selection of parts. It has been stated by some supposed to know, that on account of the comparative lack of nutrition in the Florida grasses, the breed would not admit of improvement; but from our own knowledge, and from information given us by those who have given it a fair test, we are satisfied that thoroughbreds of the Durham, Devon, Jersey, Ayrshire, Hereford and Alderney breeds can be introduced and crossed with the native stock to their marked improvement. Stock-farming of all descriptions is being generally fostered by planters as a remunerative addition to their farm interests, not only because it furnishes them with a fine quantity and quality of manure, but also because the benefits of the dairy are quite profitable in this county. We have in our mind several farms of this character, which daily supply our numerous hotels and boarding houses with milk and cream of the richest flavor. The butter also made from this milk is simply excellent, and it now bids fair to take a place among the rapidly growing industries of the many localities in this county.

But to return to the cattle industry in its largest phase. To one wholly unacquainted with this subject, or one only partially so, the manner of management and rearing would possess a peculiar interest, and as we could not in the least wise describe it more perfectly and concisely, we quote the following from the same article of Mr. Hendry's, to which we referred above: "First, the cattle owners are numerous and work in harmony for the common good, as the success of each depends upon the faithful co-operation of all. Cattle pens are erected at convenient points for gathering in the stock, always selecting localities where there is plenty of water, shade and good grazing. Our pens are built of pine logs generally, but sometimes of palmetto and cypress, and are so arranged as to have partitions for parceling into small lots or divisions. These pens are located generally from ten to fifteen miles apart, so that the herdsmen can pen their stock conveniently in whatever direction it may be found. The hunting parties generally consist of from six to ten active young men, well mounted on tough, hardy and fleet ponies. Each party has a wagon and team to transport the camp equipage and supplies, and each cow boy is prepared with a good cow whip, tin cup, wallet and saddlebags. The teamster acts in the double capacity of teamster and cook. The party generally separates from the team but one day, coming together at night. Thus equipped, the hunters start out early in the morning, the leader laying out the day's hunt, the party generally dividing into two or three sections. The leader is generally a man thoroughly conversant with the range, the marks and brands of each owner, and has the general supervision of the hunt, keeping a strict account of the supplies, the cost of the same, and also the counting and numbering the calves marked, and the beeves gathered and sold of each owner. The men are all in the saddle by sunrise in the morning, ready and anxious for their labors. The cattle are heard in the distance—the calves bleating, the cows lowing and bellowing in every direction. Orders are given to drive everything, great or small, and to pen or bring together at night all cattle found in a certain scope. The cattle are generally collected on burns, where there is plenty of green wire'grass, and are in small lots of from three to fifty head, where they are found and collected in one large drove, the gathering continued until the heat of the day, when the droves are conducted to some known spot of shade, water, etc., the cattle ready to stand quiet, and the order given to rest for two or three hours, the hunters dismount and strip their tired horses, and man and beast find refreshment. By this time a large drove of from five hundred to one thousand are collected, consisting of calves from one to two days old to the largest bulls and steers that roam the forest. When refreshed, all hands mount their horses and start the drove in the direction of the ranch or pens, moving at the rate of about one mile per hour. The herd is driven into the pens, the bars or gates are secured, and all hands, wearied, dusty, hungry and thirsty, repair to the camp . . . and after supper the horses are rubbed down, watered and fed, and turned loose on the luxuriant grass which abounds in almost every locality. . . . The marking and branding is the most laborious labor of any connected with the whole business, and it usually takes a whole day to mark, brand and regulate one of these herds. After the beef cattle are selected and separated, the calves are all marked and the herd are all turned back upon the range whence they came, and the party proceeds to repeat the same labor in other directions."

MONROE STREET, TAMPA, FLA.

The above account, which is true as well as minute, will enable you by your own calculations to arrive at the small cost of this line of business, and as the cattle trade has proven profitable in the past, so in the future will it rank high among our industries, until all the available lands in this and the other counties shall be subjected to the purposes of agriculture. The cattle men, however, are generally speaking the shrewdest men in the county, and certainly deserve encomiums for the manner in which they have trained themselves to forestall future events, and when their own interests and the good of the country require it, which, however, is yet in the future, they can and will turn their talents and attention to something else. Apart from home consumption, Key West and Cuba are our most important markets. The trade with those points was first established by Capt. James McKay, Sr., whose memory, though he has long since departed from the sorrows and trials of this life, will ever remain dear to a grateful people. We may safely say that on an average there are annually shipped to Key West and Cuba about 18,000 head of beef cattle from the five counties of Hillsborough, Polk, Manatee, Monroe and Brevard. It may seem strange, but nevertheless it is a fact admitted, that the Florida beef finds readier sale with the Cubans than heavy Texas beef; and the reason given by the Cubans is that the meat is so much more agreeable to the taste. The trade with these markets continues for about four months, commencing about the last of May and terminating some time in September or October. In reference to the gathering and herding of cattle, it strikes us that few pictures can be more pleasing and beautiful than an immense prairie covered with a fresh coat of green grass as far as the sight can reach, whose surface is dotted all over with the scattered herds like the cattle upon a thousand hills.

As to that branch of stock-raising which has sheep for its object, the very least we can say is that wherever a fair trial has been granted it, profitable results have always been experienced. We are free to admit that in those portions of the county where vegetation is comparatively sparse and coarse, while sheep will prosper on it at a fair rate, they produce an inferior quality of both wool and mutton; yet by their continued presence and under their grazing, the pine lands become enriched, and it is found that sheep and new characters of vegetation prove of mutual benefit to each other. Of course the better class of lands furnish pasturage, upon which the flocks flourish more than ordinarily well from the beginning, and the profits received from their wool and mutton give a large per cent. upon the capital invested. In comparison, we may say that notwithstanding the fact that cattle-raising has ever been a paying industry, it is thought by many that sheep will prove somewhat more profitable.

TAMPA BAY.

Sensations of utter inability, begetting the most disturbing apprehensions, fret the brain, as we propose to dwell for a few moments upon a subject which has inspired the romantic writers to their greatest and most glorious efforts. What child in all America has not had his little breast to heave with emotions of excitement and fervent gratitude, as he devoured with eagerness page after page of that pleasing little volume entitled "The Young Marooners." And it was in Tampa Bay that this family met with all their wonderful experiences and mysterious mishaps. This beautiful and magnificent expanse of water, which has often been pronounced by U. S. Coast Surveying parties to be the best harbor south of Pensacola, is wholly situated in Hillsborough county, and extends from the Gulf on the southwest for more than forty miles in a northeasterly direction, having an average width of twelve or fifteen miles. At its northern extremity a projection of land divides it into two large arms, which are commonly known as Old Tampa and Hillsborough Bays, and at the head of the latter is the present site of Tampa, which city we have already spoken of. Emptying into it from all directions are numerous interesting and highly picturesque streams, some of them taking their source from far inland, among the most important of which are the Hillsborough, Alafia and Little Manatee rivers, whose waters are navigable for small boats for many miles. A person standing upon the deck of one of the elegant steamers plowing this grand body of water at the rate of twelve or fifteen knots an hour, will be charmed and enchanted with the tropical and semi-tropical scenery which meets the gaze on every side, and many are the ejaculations of admiration and astonishment. "The forests of cabbage palmetto nodding their evergreen plumes in the morning sun, the stately date palms and olive trees on Snead's Island, on the north side of the Bay, and the pretty villas surrounded by the young orange and banana groves on the south side, form a landscape of rare tropical beauty, unexcelled in the Land of Flowers and unrivaled by the fairest scenes in Italia's famed land." The Tampa *Tribune* of recent date contains an article on Tampa Bay by Mr. S. A. Jones, which for its clear presentation of truths and a straightforward statement of facts cannot be excelled. From it we extract the following:

"Stranger, have you ever thought of a lake forty miles long and over one hundred miles of shore, and all these shores visible to the traveler of the Southern coast? This wonderful lake will and does float the largest size vessels, and also this wonderful lake has an outlet that all the trade by ships, and from all over the world, can come in her waters and find a good and safe harbor, and railroad connections to transport their cargoes to all the North and West, the only air line route from the great Bahamas, West Indies, Cuba and the South American and Caribbean ports. This beautiful lake is surrounded by a rich, healthy and fertile country, and it abounds with every kind of scale and shell fish in superabundance. This lake has bathing grounds superior to those of Saratoga, and a great and surprising thing is that its waters are warm and pleasant to bathe in from one year's end to the other. Those living along her shores are fanned by the soft salt breezes that purify the air and permeate the system with health and strength, no matter from whence the wind may blow. There are no swamps to distribute the malaria that more or less prevails in all of them. This wonderful lake assures all who settle near her shores a healthy home, and sure and cheap transportation to market for all their fruits and vegetables. Right here let me say that on the shores of this lake can be produced all kinds of tropical fruits and many of the finest and most delicate varieties that cannot be raised anywhere north of these waters. This lake has a number of feeders in the shape of navigable rivers penetrating far into the country, to induce those in the interior to raise many products on account of easy and cheap transportation to the great markets of the world. This lake has so many advantages over our sister counties' lakes that we fear to say more about it, else we may break the charm. While we do know and feel that those little inland mirrors are beautiful reflections from our great mother lake of them all, but to find a business home and pleasure home combined none can offer the inducements, convenience and facilities that we offer. This lake has not long been known to the outer world, but is now just beginning to invite people to come and air themselves in her gentle breezes. None have ever rested on her bosom that have not given her a pledge that soon they would return and cast their lots forever by her enticing shores. There is also a beautiful little city filled with live and enterprising people on the shores of this lake; a city that is destined to be the metropolis of the South. It has all the conveniences of a modern city under construction, and in a short time will be filled with people from every clime. Already the great 'medicine men' have heard of her glory as a home for the sick and feeble, and have come to discuss her merits as to the advisability of sending their sick here to be cured—not by medicines, but by the health-giving breezes that rise from this beautiful lake. And right well do they talk over the wonderful pure air that they could not believe existed until they came to see for themselves. Now there is room for many thousands on this lake, and we will welcome you to its shores. Just read the papers that go out from its shores shortly, and you will find a cheap way to come and a cheap way to stay. This is one of God's choicest blessings to the American men and women, and none should fail to come and see it. There are no great swarms of insects, and ponds of crocodiles and snakes; there are no swamps and pestilence, as has been so often told you for fear that you might come—for none have ever come who did not pledge themselves to return. For the fact is self-evident that this lake region is destined to soon be the grand winter and summer resort of the United States. It is told abroad and also in our own State, to the discredit of our neighbors of the northern and eastern parts of our State, that this great lake country is filled with cut-throats and that malaria is ever present, none of which is true; and it is a burning shame that the people visiting this State will hear people abusing all sections but the dear, beloved spot on which they live. It is either that the railroads will entirely miss this or that locality, and the absolute fact that some of our near neighbors are foolish enough to try to make strangers believe that this great lake which we speak of is to be left out entirely, and their beautiful pools are to be the great commercial centers of the State. Now we want to see a fine sanitarium and village on the banks of them, but do not try to delude the unsuspecting strangers with the idea that these little pools have anything to do with the great commerce of the world. All we ask is that all who come to Florida, take the map of our State and county, when one glance will convince you that this lake I have tried to lay before you possesses advantages possessed by none in the South; showing, beside, when the railroad gives us through lines north, we are on the only practicable air line east, west and north from the great world south of Florida. Already the enterprising men of the South Florida Railroad are fast arranging to carry the great Northern mails south through this lake and return with the sugar, tea, coffee and fruit trade of the South American ports. Soon this lake will be made a port of entry, and it is only a question of time as to when fine custom houses will be built on her shores. We will close by saying, when you start to Florida cast your eye on the map and look closely at Tampa Bay, and buy your ticket straight through. You can find all these advantages, beauties, comforts and health here, and in the fast-growing city of Tampa, beautifully located on her banks. Let those that understand read and be wise."

AN ORANGE NURSERY.

A MAMMOTH FLORIDA TREE.

EARLY VEGETABLES.

The production of early vegetables in Florida has of late years been engaged in quite extensively, and especially in the Southern counties in general and Hillsborough in particular, and their shipment to the Northern markets is assuming such enormous proportions that in time Florida will prove as famous and renowned on account of her vegetables as she is on account of her fine oranges and other fruits. It is already adjudged by those who engage in it a most important and profitable feature of her industries. It is on record that in the early season cabbages were shipped from Tallahassee, and the returns from the Northern markets to the shippers showed a net profit of $500 per acre; and since Hillsborough county is situated several hundred miles to the southward, and can and does produce almost every description of vegetables, there is no good reason why the same handsome profits cannot be realized from the shipments of this place. In South Florida more than any other section of the State, tomatoes, cucumbers and beans have been the most important articles for shipment up to the present time; but on its fertile soil peas, potatoes, cabbages and many other vegetables can be grown at seasons which will command for them fancy prices. At the lowest and most liberal calculations, it is estimated that from $400 to $700 can be easily realized on one acre of cabbage or potatoes, and such calculations are made from a few experimental shipments which were made during the past season. The profits which have accrued to the truckman from cucumbers alone are really surprising. The great difficulty which has attended this branch of Hillsborough's industries was her lack of quick and reliable transportation; but at present her facilities may be said to be fair, and the good promise of their multiplication and enlargement predicts an era in vegetable-growing in this county hitherto unknown in these Southern States. The sweet potato is the most universal, or more nearly so than any of the other vegetables, the cause, perhaps, being its easy propagation from the roots, sprouts or vines. It may be planted any season of the year, and need not be taken from the ground until required for use, except in mid-winter.

The Irish potato, or white potato, is not indigenous to these parts, but, it is said, was introduced into America by the Spaniards, from whence it was carried to England by Sir Walter Raleigh. It is more than probable that it got the name of Irish from the excellent quality of them produced in the soil of Ireland. This tuber has within late years attracted special attention, and is one of the most profitable of the early crops in Florida. On account of our mild and equable climate, this species of potato is capable of being grown from nearly one end of the year to the other, and fancy prices have been realized when they have been shipped to Northern and Eastern markets about the time the native crop is planted or exhausted. From $125 to $150 have often been realized from an acre of potatoes, and in some localities these figures have been greatly exceeded. Considerable attention is also given to the egg plant, tomatoes, onions, cabbages, peas, cucumbers, beans, squash and many others, all of which do exceedingly well and pay surprisingly. Come and try a truck farm while the orange grove grows.

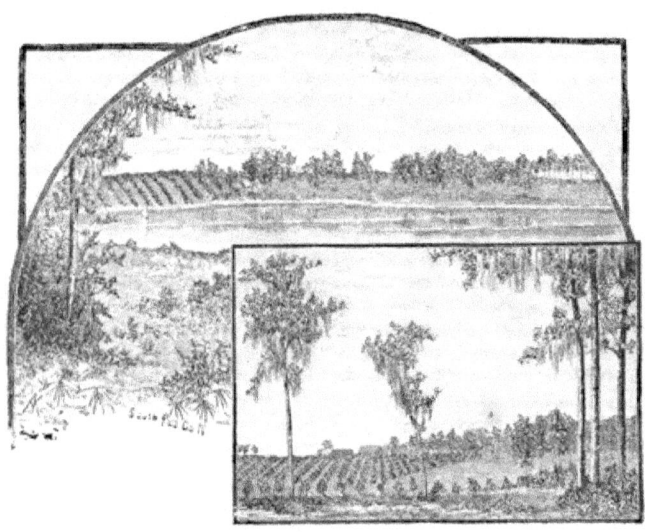

AN ORANGE GROVE AND LAKE.

EDUCATIONAL

The times demand more education and less illiteracy, and the educational system of this State, as provided by enactments of the Legislature, though it does admit of improvements in some particulars, certainly evinces a marked determination on the part of the people to meet so popular a demand. The system of Public Instruction is overlooked by a State Superintendent, assisted by a State Board of Public Instruction, a County Board of Public Instruction and County Superintendent of Education for each county, together with local trustees of each school. The numerous public schools in each county are supported by the interest of the Public School Fund, a State tax of one mill on the dollar, coupled with a county tax of not less than two and a half and not more than four mills on the dollar. The interest from the Fund and the receipts from the one-mill tax are distributed among the respective counties in proportion to the number of children ranging from four to twenty-one years of age, but they are apportioned to the schools according to the average attendance of scholars between the ages of six and twenty-one years. A teacher, in order to obtain one of these schools, must be in possession of a certificate of qualification granted by the county school board or the State Superintendent after a due examination, and these certificates are required to be renewed every year. As to the quality of schools in this county, we do not doubt but that Hillsborough can boast, since our teachers are generally paid salaries which do not, as in many of the other counties, depend entirely upon the public money which is given according to the average attendance, but are helped by private contribution or tuition, and this fact draws to us from other counties and other states a host of well-educated and well-trained teachers in search of schools, and from these we have our pick.

There are now in this county sixty-seven well-established schools, which have terms of five months every year. Besides these there are many private schools, taught by graduates of some of our best-known colleges, and in these, as well as in our public schools, the pupils are fitted for at least the ordinary pursuits of life, while in a few of a higher character sufficient education is bestowed for purposes of business and profession. The schools are all well attended, and since the teachers are not only required to stand the regular examination to show up their educational qualifications, but also to give the most satisfactory proof of their moral character, the educational advantages of this county are good and will compare very favorably with many older and more thickly settled sections of the country at large.

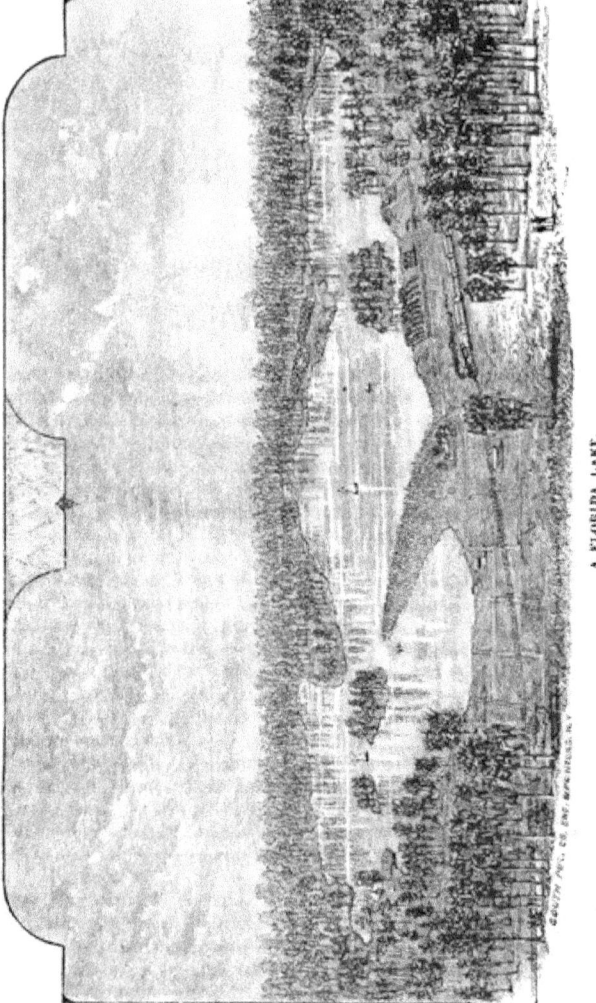

A FLORIDA LAKE.

SPONGE INTEREST.

There was a time within the memory of the present generation when all the sponges used in the United States were furnished by ships from the Mediterranean; but about the year 1852 the western coast of Florida began to attract minute and widespread attention on account of the immense numbers found in the waters along this coast, and since then sponge-fishing has been carried on all along the western coast of Florida. The fisheries are chiefly confined to the southwestern part of the coast, extending all along the shoals and reefs from St. Marks to a point off the coast of Hillsborough county, a distance of several hundred miles. At first these sponges were easily obtained from the fisherman at ten cents per pound, but as soon as it was ascertained that their quality compared favorably with those obtained from the Mediterranean, merchants began to engage in the business actively and extensively, and as those gathered in the Mediterranean began to grow scarce, their demand and value increased correspondingly.

At one time the first known fisheries on the coast of the kind under discussion began to fail, and it was then that an area of much more expanse was discovered, and which contained the most excellent quality of sponge. This discovery seemed to endow the enterprise with a new impetus, and in that and succeeding years many places along the coast fitted out vessels for the special purpose of engaging in that business. The effects of the weather upon the results of the fishing are of no small consequence, real rough weather rendering it entirely impracticable. A complete failure has been experienced in some years, but such is a very rare occurrence, and those years may be numbered upon the exceptions.

As the price of any article fluctuates according to the supply, it matters not materially whether large or small quantities are caught, the profits remaining generally about the same. The method pursued by the spongers on the Florida coast presents a striking contrast to that used in the waters of the Mediterranean. There the sponges are obtained by the fishermen diving for them. Here, small vessels containing crews of twelve or fifteen men are sent out to cruise on the sponging grounds, and on arriving upon them they divide into pairs, betaking themselves to small skiffs. One of the pair manages the skiff or "dingy," as the small boat is called, while the other leans as far over the side as possible, scanning as closely as possible the ground over which there generally is not a great many feet of water, and which is usually clear as crystal, and this is done with the aid of a common wooden bucket with a magnifying-glass bottom, which is put over the water and the face thrust as far into it as convenient. As soon as a sponge is spied the boat is brought to an immediate stand-still as near as possible by a dextrous use of the oars, and the sponge then secured by means of a two-pronged iron hook fastened to the end of a long pole. No small amount of skill and care is required of both of the men in the boat. The preparation of the sponge for market is also an interesting feature. They are placed along the deck of the vessel in an upright position, in order that they may defunct in a natural position, and while decomposition is transpiring allow the gelatinous matter to escape freely. They are then thrown into pens of water built along the shore, where the remaining matter is soaked and pressed out. From May until August is considered the principal season for these cruises, but even in the winter months it has been carried on with surprising success. We would not even unwittingly praise any enterprise beyond its just deserts; neither would we do so for selfish reasons; but we verily believe there is a remunerative field open to a live man in the sponge fishing, and with Tampa as convenient headquarters, many vessels might be profitably engaged in that trade off the west coast of this county.

STREET SCENE IN A SOUTH FLORIDA TOWN.

CLIMATE AND HEALTH OF HILLSBOROUGH.

The climate of Florida is so generally understood throughout every section of the civilized world that the reader would indeed have just cause to complain of our taxing his patience did we propose to be very prodigal in our observations upon it; and to be frank upon this subject, we would remain silent, were it not so closely connected with the health. It is not a hot climate in summer, but on the contrary is mild and subject to very few atmospheric changes.

The winters are neither cold nor freezing, but uniformly cool and bracing, and during the whole year the cloudy and disagreeable days may be regarded as the exceptions, fair, bright and sunny days being the general rule. We recognize that the summer is longer, but the heat is less oppressive than mid-summer at the North, which fact you can gather from the following meteorology, which we extract from a pamphlet published by Dr. Wall:

"Tampa, being nearly centrally situated on the Gulf coast, and some thirty miles interiorly from the Gulf at the head of Hillsborough Bay, is selected as a fair medium locality for the following meteorological observations. These are taken from the statistical report of the Surgeon General's Office, published in 1856: The mean temperature for the seasons and for the whole year for twenty-five years is, spring, 72 deg. 08 min.; summer, 80 deg. 20 min.; autumn, 71 deg. 04 min.; winter, 62 deg. 35 min.; whole year, 72 deg. 48 min. The mean rainfall for the seasons and for the whole year for sixteen years is, spring, 8.56 inches; summer, 28.24 inches; autumn, 10.63 inches; winter, 8.04 inches; whole year, 55.47 inches. The following summary of the weather is the mean for nine years. (The capitals indicate the direction of the wind, and the figures the numbers of days from that direction.) N., 27; N.E., 73; E., 69; S.E., 44; S., 40; S.W., 43; W., 43; N.W., 29; fair, 245; cloudy, 143; rainy, 98."

For days together New York, Boston and other Northern places show in summer temperature as high as 100 degrees; it is very seldom that it ever reaches that degree in Florida for a single day, generally ranging below 90 degrees. The atmosphere is not oppressive, sultry, close or humid, but the mornings and evenings are always cool and refreshing. As to the diseases, we quote from Dr. Wall again in his same publication. He says that the endemic diseases only comprise those of malarial origin, such as intermittent and remittent fever, and of those the types are mild, the pernicious and malignant cases being the exceptions.

Of the continued fevers, such as typhoid and typho-malarial, not a case has occurred within an experience of fifteen years. This will be a fact of important significance to those who recall the scourging devastation of typhoid fever at the North and West. In a residence of seventeen years in Tampa, yellow fever made its appearance once, which was in 1871; since that time Tampa has been entirely free from its visitation, while Jacksonville, Fernandina and Pensacola have not, a fact which goes to prove that the people of this section are alive to the needs of good quarantine regulations and also to a good internal sanitary condition. The dengue makes occasional visits to this section, and while it is very painful, mortality is a very seldom consequence. This disease first made its appearance in Philadelphia, having been imported from the West Indies. Both the yellow fever and the dengue can be as easily stamped out in the Southern as in the Northern cities, since it is not endemic but an exotic. The yellow fever has existed as an epidemic as high north as Portland, Maine.

Idiopathic diseases of the liver, with the exception of an occasional case of jaundice, are unknown to Dr. Wall, and are very uncommon. "Acute inflammatory affections of the respiratory organs—except an occasional catarrh, with some bronchitis—are extremely infrequent as a rule, though here, as elsewhere, an epidemic influenza sometimes prevails, during which serious pulmonary complications in some cases are developed, taking their departure apparently from the epidemic disease. But idiopathic pneumonia and pleurisy occur very rarely, and are never so common as to be considered as even approximating an endemic or an epidemic character. Diarrhœa and dysentery only occur as sporadic diseases, and never in an epidemic or malignant form. These diseases are generally mild, and readily yield to treatment. No case of acute rheumatism has ever come under my observation, except when the patient was also suffering with a gonorrhœal discharge more or less acute."

Cerebro-spinal meningitis, whether as sporadic or epidemic, is unknown in the State south of Ocala, where it is said to have prevailed in the winter of 1863-4. Traumatic tetanus occurs but very infrequently after wounds or injuries, and the Doctor further declares that this section has escaped diphtheria, though there are not wanting physicians here, as everywhere, who, either from ignorance or an unprofessional anxiety for reputation, call almost every affection of the throat diphtheria. Insolation or sunstroke never occurs in either town or country. No instance of hydrophobia, in either animal or human, within the State has come within our knowledge. The mortality of this section is extremely low, and that from malarial fevers for the last few years has been nil, and so far as statistics can be made available they show a less percentage of mortality than any other State in the Union. The entire absence of many diseases more or less fatal in their character, and the greater mildness of those of malarial origin, cannot fail to demonstrate the natural salubrity of the climate. Much of this exemption from the graver forms of disease depends doubtless upon its greater freedom from the extremes of temperature.

We have thus quoted rather fully from this valuable pamphlet, not only because of our appreciation of its intrinsic value, but also because of our own inability to treat so difficult a subject in the scientific manner it properly merits. Out of justice to Dr. Wall, we think it highly proper for us to state the year of its publication, which was some time in 1874.

CONCLUSION

In concluding these pages upon a section of country which is favored with all the natural advantages and facilities for so many of the callings of life, we wish it to be remembered that we have endeavored to steer clear of all exaggerations, and we have endeavored to set forth nothing except such facts and opinions as are justified by experience, observation and study. We are frank in our confessions that these pages are intended to attract people to our midst who will help to swell our population and take advantage of our many unbounded resources; but, nevertheless, we have confined ourselves to the path of truth and honesty, which fact will manifest itself to you upon your arrival among us, for you will then see that there are many attractions which we have not even mentioned, and that those of which we have taken notice are not painted as vividly and glowingly as a just and fair estimate warrants. By a careful perusal you have no doubt observed that we have tenaciously clung to our purpose not to place intentionally any other section of our beloved State in an unfavorable light, nor have we in the least intended to disparage any of our sister counties by close comparisons with our present subject, for it has not been our object, nor will it ever be, to praise our own section to the detriment and damage of another. Come among us, and by our congeniality and hospitality we will try to cause you to think of us as friends and old acquaintances; few of us are "natives to the manner born," for we are either immigrants ourselves or the offspring of immigrants. We do not invite any to come into our midst who have the mistaken idea deep down in the recesses of their hearts that here people are exempt from that inexorable rule, "in the sweat of thy brow thou shalt eat bread," and that money grows on trees, or that full-bearing orange groves and fruit farms spring into existence simply because one will settle in Florida; on the contrary, instead of advising such to come, we advise them to stay away, for we want no such fools. Florida is good and great enough in all her advantages, and God Almighty has in a wonderful way blessed Hillsborough county, but if you allow imagination to run away with you and to paint in glowing colors wondrous things to be accomplished in this sunny clime of ours outside of the pale of common human effort, you will be greatly disappointed when you come. So we say, try to be practical in your ideas, and keep yourself on a plane of human life and earthly countries. We desire all who will do this to come and live among us, for here you can be healthy, prosperous and happy.

We not only wish the rich and independent with their capital to come, but also those of the humbler walks of life, for Hillsborough county needs one as much as the other, and offers to the poor and rich alike opportunities of the rarest kind. We wish you to fill no subordinate places, except from choice, for if you are scarce in pocket, the cheapness of our many vacant lands and the easy terms upon which they can be purchased will admit of your becoming proprietors in fee simple. And especially do we want those of an agricultural and horticultural turn of mind, so that the cultivation of our early vegetables may receive the attention and development they deserve. Mechanics and skilled artisans we wish also, for there is no vocation among us which does not admit of greater attention and development. Most earnestly do we insist upon those coming who have capital for investment, for we wish to see all our resources put upon the footing which their merit and greatness commands. In fact, there are none but the lethargic and inert whom we do not want to come and identify themselves with us.

We are satisfied that you understand our invitation well enough now for us to draw these imperfect pages to a close sayiby ng that if you come into our midst, the full right hand of every citizen in Hillsborough county will be extended to you in honest and sincere friendship, so we say in farewell, Come one, come all, and see what the Lord hath done for us.

AVENUE BORDERING ORANGE GROVE.

APPENDIX.

Since the foregoing was written and arranged, several matters of no small importance have attracted our attention, and out of common justice to them it is necessary that they be at least mentioned and briefly noticed. At this juncture, also, we would beg the indulgence of the patient reader while we express our deep regrets that shortness of time and unfavorable circumstances have prevented the insertion of statistics in any of the branches of business, both mercantile and otherwise. However, by a careful perusal, you have acquired sufficient information to permit of your arriving at an approximate estimate of these and other things of peculiar moment.

By our seeming negligence, one of the most praiseworthy features of Tampa was on the verge of being omitted, for very recently a Board of Trade was organized, and its actions already convince the veriest pessimist that by organizations of that character much more can be accomplished than by the non-co-operative efforts of individuals with their petitions and prayers. We have examined the constitution and by-laws of this association, and as one of its many objects is to foster, encourage and develop the mercantile, manufacturing and other interests of Tampa and its suburbs, it has and will retain the sympathies and assistance of every class of the citizens. Already it has put on foot a movement which in all probability will give us within a reasonable length of time street-cars through all the principal thoroughfares out into convenient parts of the vicinity; but its many determinate purposes we find ourselves unable to consider.

Another item of significance is in reference to a Journal which will be published by the Hillsborough County Real Estate Agency, and beyond even the shadow of a doubt its proposed system of advertisement and general management is simply unique. This Journal will be called the Tampa *Courier*, and in the sincere and honest opinion of the writer (apart from all other considerations), its advertising advantages are of such a nature that it will afford opportunities which have never before been in the reach of any section of Florida. The writer speaks not without sufficient knowledge.

The following letter was received a few days previous to the present writing, and as it speaks for itself, we simply append without any comments:

To ————————

        Dear Sir:

                Mr. S. A. Jones informs me that in the descriptive article you are writing for the Hillsborough County Real Estate Agency you will want to mention the various branches of business, insurance with the others; and to enable you to say what you desire on this subject, I submit the following data:

The following fire insurance companies are represented in Tampa and Hillsborough county by Thos. A. Carruth, agent:

Home, of New York; Continental, of New York; New York Underwriters' Agency; Hartford Fire, of Hartford, Conn.; Liverpool and London and Globe; Springfield Fire and Marine, of Springfield, Mass.; Providence Washington, of Providence, R. I., and New Orleans Insurance Association, of New Orleans, La. Also the Travelers' Life and Accident, of Hartford, Conn., and the Equitable Life Insurance Association, of New York. Thos. A. Carruth, agent, and Dr. John P. Wall, medical examiner.

Respectfully,

THOS. A. CARRUTH.

ALACHUA SINK, FLORIDA.

MR. WM. A. MORRISON'S VILLA AT TAMPA.

A LAKE SCENE.

JNO. T. LESLEY,   F. A. JONES,   LAWSON CHASE,   GEO. T. CHAMBERLAIN,
President.   Gen'l. Manager.   Secretary   Treasurer.

HILLSBOROUGH COUNTY

REAL * ESTATE * AGENCY

TAMPA, FLORIDA.

This Agency offers the best and most complete facilities to buyers or settlers, of any Agency in South Florida. We are prepared to give you the cheapest and most desirable routes to come to Florida, and special facilities for locating here. We have lands and property of every description to suit the wants of all classes. Wild land for colonies, improved lands, houses, groves, plantations, truck-farms, etc., on creeks, rivers, lakes and bays for private parties. Town lots and town houses in all the towns in this county. Valuable lands, groves, farms, etc., in all of the adjoining counties.

We locate lands, look after homesteads, contract for and superintend improvements, pay taxes, perfect titles, secure abstracts, procure deeds and look after and attend to any and all kinds of business in our line, entrusted to us. Furnish any information relating to this part of Florida to any and all seeking homes to settle on, or for investment among us. This agency will make loans for parties desiring to place money in Florida; obtain paying rate of interest and guarantee ample and safe securities.

We are a chartered company, and besides being responsible, are amenable to the laws of the State that granted us our charter. So all who contract with us or entrust their funds to us can feel safe and sure of fair dealing and protection in their trusts, and not being speculated on. We do not speculate; but buy and sell, strictly, on commission. We take property at a price. We sell at that price. All of our transactions are regularly recorded, and our books are our and your protection and proof. This is our home. It is the most desirable part of Florida. We want it known. We want to build it up and are working to that end. We publish to this end and with this aim one of the largest papers in South Florida. Send us your address. Come and see us and we promise you "the best the market affords."

WM. B. BAKER, PRES.   ROBT. A. HINTZE, TREAS.   ROBT. B. FARSON, SEC'Y.

—THE—

✥ HINTZE & BAKER COMPANY, ✲

Manufacturers of

SASH, DOORS, BLINDS, MOULDINGS,

STAIR WORK, Etc.

LUMBER ST., COR. TWENTY SECOND,

CHICAGO, ILL.

RAILROAD ✲ LANDS,

In Putnam, Marion, Alachua, Hernando, Polk, and Hillsborough Counties.

LANDS OF ALL CLASSES AND GRADES, ON RIVERS AND RAILROADS, AT PRICES RANGING FROM $2.50 TO $10 PER ACRE.

ADDRESS

 S. I. WAILES,

Land Commissioner,

FLORIDA RAILWAY AND NAVIGATION COMPANY,

108 West Bay Street, Jacksonville, Fla.

P. O. BOX 723.

ARE YOU INTERESTED IN FLORIDA?

―― IF SO ――

——SUBSCRIBE——

―― FOR THE ――

SOUTH FLORIDA COURIER,

PUBLISHED AT

PLANT CITY, FLORIDA.

The *Courier* is an eight-column, four-page weekly newspaper, devoted to the interests of Florida in general and Hillsborough county and Plant City in particular.

Terms: $2.00 per Year; Six Months, $1.00.

Democratic in politics—but politics are secondary to our aims and purposes of building up and developing this favored section of the world.

SAMPLE COPIES SENT ON APPLICATION.

F. W. MERRIN & SONS, PROPRIETORS

J. D. CLARKE & CO.,

— DEALERS IN —

DRY * GOODS,

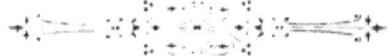

BOOTS, SHOES AND HATS AND GENTS' FURNISHING GOODS.

Also Light Groceries. Shoes a Specialty.

TAMPA, FLORIDA.

JOHN F. BROWNING,
— AGENT —

DOMESTIC AND WHITE SEWING MACHINES,
TAMPA, FLORIDA.

FOURTEEN YEARS' EXPERIENCE.

After a close application to business for a number of years, in machines, I can safely say that I am now offering to the public superior machines and on better terms than they have ever had before.

The Domestic and White, two of the best machines now in use, both with new and elegant wood-work, new steel sets of attachments and attached to the machines without the use of screw or screw driver, and so simple and practical that a child ten years old can tuck, fell, cord, bind, puff, plait, shirr and gather with perfect ease.

If you have an old machine, exchange it for a Domestic or White. Call and see or write for circulars. All kinds of machine needles, oils and attachments generally.

Washington Street, next door to E. A. Clarke & Co., Tampa, Fla.

J. F. BROWNING,
— AGENT —

THE TAMPA TRIBUNE,

TAMPA, FLA.

Terms of Subscription. $2.00 Per Annum.

THE TRIBUNE is regarded by all as one of the most reliable papers in the State, and is devoted to the encouragement of immigration and the development of the vast resources of the Peninsular portion of Florida, consisting of the Counties of Hillsborough, Hernando, Polk, Manatee, and the Caloosahatchie region of Monroe. It has a large and increasing circulation in all the Counties bordering on the Gulf, and is therefore the

BEST ✦ ADVERTISING ✦ MEDIUM ✦ IN ✦ SOUTH ✦ FLORIDA.

TAMPA

is the largest town on the mainland in South Florida, and located at the head of Hillsborough Bay, a subdivision of Tampa Bay, which is the largest bay and best harbor on the Gulf Coast of the Peninsula. Tampa is the terminus of the South Florida Railroad and also of several projected railways whose construction will be consummated at no distant day. Steamers ply regularly between Tampa and Key West, Havana, New Orleans, Cedar Key and all points on Tampa Bay and the Manatee River. The hotels are large and commodious; the markets are supplied with the best fish, oysters and other salt water delicacies, and in less than twelve months the town will be protected against fire by the Holly system of water works.

Address all communications relating to subscriptions or advertisements to

SPENCER & SCALES,

TAMPA, FLA.

E. A. CLARKE.   A. J. KNIGHT.

E. A. CLARKE & CO.,

ESTABLISHED 1854.

One of the oldest established firms in South Florida—and we proudly refer to our long standing and present status in the mercantile world, as a proof of our worth and popularity with our people.

During the times that "tried men's souls" we were of the people and with the people, and endeavoring to give them dollar for dollar. We are yet laboring in the same line.

Every body knows us and our location. Every body knows we deal in

✷ GENERAL MERCHANDISE ✷

and keep on hand everything a first-class store should keep; and every body knows our

PRICES ARE REASONABLE,

and if any one should ask why then do we advertise at all? We say, because we don't want it all, but want to give the papers a chance. We will always be glad to see you. Give us a call.

E. A. CLARKE & CO.,

TAMPA, FLORIDA.

SUNNNYSIDE NURSERY,

FORT MEADE, FLA.

ORANGE TREES OF ALL SIZES AND VARIETIES ON HAND

Budded fruits and flowers a specialty. Everything delivered to most distant points in perfect condition.

THE HILLSBOROUGH COUNTY REAL ESTATE AGENCY

ARE MY AUTHORIZED AGENTS.

Prices cheerfully furnished.

C. L. MITCHELL,

FORT MEADE, FLA.

L. S. Dawes, Dillingham & Co.

TAMPA IRON FOUNDRY

SOMETHING NEW.

The only Iron Foundry South of Jacksonville.

All kinds of Work in our line promptly attended to. Patronage Solicited.

C. W. ANDREWS,

✢ NOTARY PUBLIC STATE AT LARGE, ✢

—AND—

DEALER IN REAL ESTATE.

PLANT CITY, HILLSBOROUGH CO., FLA.

I offer the lands of the Florida Land and Mortgage Company, and the Florida Land and Improvement Company, at graded prices, on time and for cash. I have the finest farming lands near Plant City, to be found in Florida at low prices; orange groves, improved places, residences, lots of 5 and 10 acres etc., and offer a large list to select from. Lands bought for non-residents, taxes paid, groves kept up and improvements made and titles examined. Correspondence solicited. Strangers are invited to call at my office, where they will be courteously received.

WILLIAM M. BIRD & CO.,

201 East Bay Street. Charleston. S. C.

—— DEALERS IN ——

PAINTS AND PAINTERS' MATERIAL

of all Descriptions.

RAILROAD, STEAMBOAT AND MILL SUPPLIES,

SHIP CHANDLERY, ETC.

—— AGENTS FOR ——

MARVIN'S SAFES AND HOWE'S SCALES.

Price Lists & Sample Cards Furnished on Application.

DOORS, SASH, BLINDS

and Builders' Hardware, Wholesale and Retail.

GEO. F. DREW & CO.,

Jacksonville. Fla.

✹ MECHANICS' TOOLS AND FARMING IMPLEMENTS. ✹

—— SOLE AGENTS FOR THE STATE OF ——

Buckthorn Barb Wire, Herring's Safes, Buffalo Scales,
Longman & Martinez Prepared Paints.

STEAMBOAT & MILL SUPPLIES A SPECIALTY.

—— We carry on an extensive ——

Plumbing. Gas and Steam Fitting and Tin Shop.

THOMAS A. GARRETH.
INSURANCE AGENT, TAMPA, FLORIDA.

———REPRESENTING———

Home Insurance Co. (Fire), of New York	Assets,	$7,395,090 55
Continental Insurance Co. (Fire), of New York	"	4,998,501 92
New York Underwriters' Agency, N. Y.	"	3,647,180 48
Liverpool and London and Globe Insurance Co.	"	5,771,959 71
Hartford Fire Insurance Co., Hartford, Conn.	"	4,491,880 01
Springfield Fire and Marine Insurance Co., Springfield, Mass.	"	2,562,510 29
Providence Washington Insurance Co., Providence, R. I.	"	879,950 87
New Orleans Insurance Association, New Orleans, La.	"	880,351 50
The Traveler's Life and Accident, Hartford, Conn.	"	7,826,450 80
Equitable Life Insurance Association, New York	"	58,161,925 54
Aggregate of assets		$96,195,797 71

All classes of insurable property or lives in any portion of Hillsborough county placed at standard rates.

J. * J. * BOYETT,
REAL * ESTATE * AGENT
AND NOTARY PUBLIC STATE AT LARGE,

Has in his hands for sale, $175,000 worth of improved real estate, consisting of Orange Groves of all ages and sizes; also unimproved land of any amount. Prices from $1.25 to $150 per acre. Will locate Homesteads and improve groves for non-residents. For further information, address me at

PERU, HILLSBOROUGH COUNTY, FLORIDA.

GEO. B. WEEDON, M. D.   F. GHIRA.

WEEDON & GHIRA.
———DEALERS IN———
DRUGS AND MEDICINES,
PAINTS, OILS AND TOILET ARTICLES.
— TAMPA, FLORIDA.—

PEOPLE'S JEWELRY STORE,
CORNER FRANKLIN AND JACKSON STREETS.
TAMPA, FLORIDA.

A fine stock of Watches, Clocks, Jewelry and Optical Goods constantly on hand. Rare Florida Birds, Sea Shells, Sea Beans, coral, etc. The finest collection of Florida Souvenirs to be seen in the state. Orders by mail or otherwise promptly filled. Fine watchwork, and the fitting of the eyes a specialty. Satisfaction guaranteed. Eyes tested without charge.

——— C. L. AYRES, PROPRIETOR.

CRAFT HOUSE.

Quiet Locality. Large, Airy Rooms.

First-class Private Boarding House.

Terms, $2 per day. Apply to

MRS. EMMA M. CRAFT,

TAMPA, FLORIDA.

GENERAL BUSINESS AGENCY

OF

W. N. CONOLLY,

TAMPA, FLORIDA.

Any and all business attended to promptly. Collections made; Deeds, Mortgages and Contracts drawn at short notice. Special attention given to land matters of all kinds. Correspondence solicited.

GREAVES & BURTON,

MANGO, FLORIDA.

J. Q. BURTON,

PHYSICIAN AND DRUGGIST,

Deals in everything usually kept in a

FIRST-CLASS DRUG STORE.

WM. B. LYNCH.   N. P. BISHOFF.

SAN ANTONIO,

HERNANDO COUNTY, FLORIDA.

THE AMERICAN ITALY!

Fine Lands! Pure Water! Health Unexcelled!

Many acres of beautiful land, improved and unimproved, in this charming section of the land of Flowers are now offered for sale by us. For all information in regard to the same, address—

LYNCH & BISHOFF, REAL ESTATE AGENTS,

SAN ANTONIO, FLORIDA.

APPLY TO THIS AGENCY FOR ANYTHING REFERRING TO LAND OR INVESTMENTS.

If you want a home in Florida apply to this Agency. Facilities unsurpassed by any in the State.

THE TAMPA GUARDIAN.
TAMPA, FLA.

"Neutral in Nothing; Independent in Everything."

TWO DOLLARS A YEAR.

THE GUARDIAN is in its 11th volume. It gives newsier, fresher, more and better reading matter than any paper in this section.

H. J. COOPER,
EDITOR AND MANAGER.

BRANCH'S * OPERA * HOUSE.

The largest and finest Public Hall in South Florida.

SEATING CAPACITY OF AUDITORIUM AND GALLERY, 800.

—ADDRESS—

H. L. BRANCH,
——TAMPA, FLORIDA.——

S. P. HAYDEN,
LIVERY, SALE AND FEED
STABLE.

Teams at any and all times. Stables at the

HAYDEN * FERRY.
Also Dealer in General Merchandise.

TAMPA, FLA.

Write to this Agency for information on the best and cheapest route to this part of Florida. You can save money by it.

FLORIDA FERTILIZING COMPANY.
"FLORIDA ORANGE FOOD."

This Company has been organized by orange growers of Florida, for the purpose of procuring a reliable Fertilizer at a reasonable price, and one especially adapted to orange trees and suitable to our sandy soils. It has been tested in Florida for the past five years, and will prevent the scale insect, and has been tested alongside of the high-priced fertilizers, and has been found superior to any, as its lasting effects have been shown for two years. It is purely mineral, and contains no ammonia. It has a very large quantity of potash and phosphoric acid, the ingredients most required by the orange tree.

ANALYSIS.

Bone phosphate of lime, 20 per cent.; phosphoric acid, 10 per cent.; sulphate potash, 12 per cent.; magnesia, 6 per cent.; sulphur, 5 per cent. Price, $23 per ton.

"Florida Vegetable Food" containing 3 per cent. of ammonia, $28 per ton.

For circulars with full description send to

E. T. PAINE, PRESIDENT,
JACKSONVILLE, FLORIDA.

BUY YOUR TICKETS IN JACKSONVILLE,
Via East Tennessee, Virginia, Georgia Railroad, North and South, from the courteous and popular agent,

B. H. HOPKINS.

You will find him equal to all emergencies, and ready to assist all who travel by the popular route he represents.

OFFICE, CORNER HOGAN AND BAY STREETS,
JACKSONVILLE, FLORIDA.

HEADQUARTERS FOR FLORIDA FRUIT IN CHARLESTON, S. C.
C. BART & CO.,
IMPORTERS OF
FOREIGN FRUIT
AND COMMISSION MERCHANTS.
55, 57 & 59 MARKET STREET,
CHARLESTON, S. C.,

Respectfully offer their services to the growers of Florida, for the sale of Oranges, Melons and Vegetables. References: First National, and People's National Bank, Charleston, S. C., and Chemical National Bank, New York.

C. FLOYD,
— DEALER IN —
WINES, WHISKEY AND CIGARS,
DRAUGHT BEER A SPECIALTY.
TAMPA, FLORIDA.

APPLY TO THIS AGENCY FOR ANYTHING REFERRING TO LAND OR INVESTMENTS.

If you want a home in Florida apply to this agency. Facilities unsurpassed by any in the State.

J. C. FIELD,
PORTRAIT AND LANDSCAPE
PHOTOGRAPHER.

Views of Tampa and vicinity for sale.

OLD PICTURES COPIED AND ENLARGED.

BOX 225, TAMPA, FLORIDA.

MRS. F. C. BINKLEY,

✶ LADIES' FURNISHING GOODS, ✶

NEXT TO OPERA HOUSE.

TAMPA, FLORIDA.

HERMAN GLOWGOSKI,

DEALER IN

CLOTHING AND GENTS' FURNISHING GOODS,

BOOTS AND SHOES, HATS AND CAPS,

TAMPA, FLORIDA.

Write to this Agency for information on the best and cheapest route to this part of Florida. You can save money.

If you want a home in Florida apply to this Agency. Facilities unsurpassed by any in the State.

Apply to this Agency for anything referring to land or investments.

W. K. WINGATE,
Miller & Henderson Block, Tampa, Fla.
GENERAL MERCHANDISE
—AND—
FANCY GROCERY STORE.
DEALER IN VEGETABLES AND COUNTRY PRODUCE.

W. G. FERRIS,
—DEALER IN—
GENERAL MERCHANDISE,
WHOLESALE AND RETAIL,
CORNER OF WASHINGTON AND MONROE STREETS.
TAMPA, FLORIDA.

JOHN T. LESLEY & CO.,
TAMPA, FLORIDA.
DRUGGISTS, PHARMACISTS
—AND DEALERS IN—
DRUGS, MEDICINES AND CHEMICALS.
Fancy and Toilet Articles, Sponges, Brushes, Perfumery and Cigars.
Physicians' Prescriptions Accurately Compounded.
Physicians and country dealers will find our stock complete and prices as low as any in the State. All orders will receive careful and prompt attention. Satisfaction guaranteed.

Write to this Agency for information on the best and cheapest route to this part of Florida. You can save money by it.

APPLY TO THIS AGENCY FOR ANYTHING REFERRING TO LAND OR INVESTMENTS.

If you want a home in Florida apply to this Agency. Facilities unsurpassed by any in the State.

⊲KIBBEE HOUSE⊳
RESTAURANT AND BOARDING.
—— NICE AIRY ROOMS.——
NEXT TO THE OPERA HOUSE.
—— TAMPA, FLORIDA.——

TIVOLA SALOON,
Sample Room and Billiard Parlor,
Jackson Street, one door west of Franklin.
—— TAMPA, FLORIDA.——
WM. H. WEBB, PROPRIETOR.

Always on hand, the finest brands of Brandies, Whiskies, Gins, Wines, Beer and Cigars. Fancy Drinks, compounded by an experienced compounder of drinks and beverages, a specialty. Give him a call.

J. P. ANDREW,
WHOLESALE DEALER IN——
FINE LIQUORS, WINES, CIGARS.
FANCY BAR AND BILLIARD HALL.
AN ORDERLY HOUSE KEPT.
—— TAMPA, FLORIDA.——

Write to this Agency for information on the best and cheapest route to this part of Florida. You can save money by it.

APPLY TO THIS AGENCY FOR ANYTHING REFERRING TO LAND OR INVESTMENTS.

If you want a home in Florida apply to this Agency. Facilities unsurpassed by any in the State.

A. PREVATT & CO.,

Dealers in all kinds of

FISH, ✻ OYSTERS, ✻ FRUIT, ✻ VEGETABLES

AND POULTRY,

TAMPA, FLORIDA.

ORDERS PROMPTLY ATTENDED TO.

"STEWART" JACKSON,

Who has had thirty years' experience as "Steamboat Cook," keeps a first-class

RESTAURANT

MEALS AT ALL HOURS.

CAMPBELL BLOCK,

TAMPA, FLORIDA.

RESTAURANT AND ICE CREAM PARLOR,

LAFAYETTE ST., NEAR TAMPA ST.

FIRST-CLASS IN ALL APPOINTMENTS

The undersigned have opened the above place, which will be kept in first-class style in every respect, and open the year round. Special attention will be given to the table, which will be supplied with the best the market affords, and meals served at all hours. Ice Cream, Iced Tea, Milk, cool drinks and confectioneries always on hand, and families or parties supplied on short notice.

J. M. EDDINS & TINDOLPH, PROPRIETORS,

TAMPA, FLORIDA.

Write to this Agency for information on the best and cheapest route to this part of Florida. You can save money.

APPLY TO THIS AGENCY FOR ANYTHING REFERRING TO
LAND OR INVESTMENTS.

If you want a home in Florida apply to this agency. Facilities unsurpassed by any in the State.

PLANT CITY.

W. F. BURTS & CO.,
Wholesale and Retail Dealer in
GROCERIES, HARDWARE,
GRAIN, HAY AND PRODUCE.

Produce taken in exchange for goods. Give us a call.

PLANT CITY, FLORIDA.

PEMBERTON & ROBERTS,
DEALERS IN
DRY GOODS, GROCERIES,
FURNITURE AND GENERAL MERCHANDISE.
PLANT CITY, FLORIDA.

We carry a full and heavy stock, and sell at the lowest cash prices. Buy from us and SAVE MONEY.

COLLINS & FRANKLIN,
THE OLD RELIABLE
Dry Goods and Grocery House,
Keep constantly a full supply of
GENERAL MERCHANDISE.

The first established house in
PLANT CITY, FLORIDA.

Write to this Agency for information on the best and cheapest route to this part of Florida. You can save money by it.

R. B. McLENDON. W. H. YOUNG.

McLendon & Young,

REAL * ESTATE * AGENTS,

PLANT CITY, FLORIDA.

If you want a bearing orange grove or a nice young grove, unimproved farming or gardening lands in the vicinity of this young and rapidly growing town, which is situated in Hillsborough—the best county in the State for growing all tropical and semi-tropical fruits, vegetables, sugar cane, corn, oats, rye, peas, potatoes, (Irish and sweet,) and other things too numerous to mention, now is the time to buy. We have several nice residences, also business and residence lots in town which we are offering low, for cash, if sold soon.

We have good vehicles and will take pleasure in showing you our country, free of charge. Correspondence solicited. See article on Plant City.

Apply to this Agency for anything referring to land or investments.

AUGUST PETERSON,

Sign and Ornamental

PAINTER AND GRAINER,

Paper Hanger and House Fitter.

Satisfaction Guaranteed.

TAMPA, FLORIDA.

R. M. WELLS, M. D.,

PHYSICIAN AND SURGEON,

PLANT CITY, FLORIDA.

F. P. SECLOR,

DRUGGIST & PHARMACIST,

Dealer in

Drugs, Chemicals, Fancy and Toilet Articles, etc.

TAMPA, FLORIDA.

R. B. McLENDON,

Proprietor

PLANT CITY HOTEL.

Accommodations good, and board at reasonable rates.

PLANT CITY, FLORIDA.

M. E. HAYNSWORTH,

TINNER AND JOBBER GENERALLY.

Keeps constantly on hand Cooking and Warming Stoves, Roof-flanges of different pitch for side or comb of roof, and stove-piping of all sizes and kinds. House Furnishing Tins, such as Valleys and Flashings; also Shingle Tins.

Roofing and Guttering a Specialty.

TAMPA, FLORIDA.

J. B. ROBINSON,

Proprietor

ROBINSON HOUSE.

Board by the day or week at reasonable rates; accommodations good.

Give us a trial.

PLANT CITY, FLORIDA.

Write to this Agency for information on the best and cheapest route to this part of Florida. You can save money by it.

Apply to this Agency for anything referring to land or investments.

W. J. MORSE,

ARCHITECT AND BUILDER,

TAMPA, FLORIDA.

LEO. TAUFKIRCH,

BUILDER AND CONTRACTOR,

TAMPA, FLORIDA.

DR. J. A. GIDDENS,

❋ DENTIST. ❋

Graduate of Pennsylvania College, Philadelphia.

Gas administered.

Office over Macfarlane & Cleaveland's Shoe Store.

TAMPA, FLORIDA.

DR. DUFF POST,

❋ DENTIST. ❋

Office Hours

9 A. M. to 12 M., and 2 to 5 P. M.

Office over Leonardi & Co's Drug Store,

TAMPA, FLORIDA.

DR. M. M. HILL,

PHYSICIAN AND SURGEON.

Office over Leonardi's Drug Store,

TAMPA, FLORIDA.

HAMPTON & JONES,

REAL ESTATE AGENTS.

TAMPA, FLORIDA.

Write to this Agency for information on the best and cheapest route to this part of Florida. You can save money by it.

Apply to this Agency for anything referring to land or investments.

PETTINGILL & CO.,

STATIONERY,

School and Blank Books, Wall Paper, Pictures and Frames, Stationers' Specialties of all sorts at wholesale and retail. Circulating Library.

Franklin Street.

TAMPA, FLORIDA.

J. H. WELLS,

MACHINE SHOP.

All kinds of Mill Supplies furnished and all kinds of repairing in iron and steel done on short notice.

TAMPA, FLORIDA.

J. T. GUNN & CO.

Wholesale and Retail Dealers in Staple and Fancy

GROCERIES,

Flour, Grits, Meal and Bacon, etc.

TAMPA, FLORIDA.

MRS. S. D. VAUGHAN,

Ladies' Hats, Hosiery, Shoes, etc. Dresses made to order.

MILLINERY,

Fancy and Dress Goods.

TAMPA, FLORIDA.

HERMANN & WEISSBROD,

Manufacturers of

SADDLES AND HARNESS.

Repairing nicely and cheaply done.

Buggies nicely recovered.

TAMPA, FLORIDA.

C. L. FRIEBELE.

Old Reliable

GENERAL MERCHANDISE.

House established in 1858.

TAMPA, FLORIDA.

Write to this Agency for information on the best and cheapest route to this part of Florida. You can save money by it.

PROFESSIONAL PAGE.

HAMMOND & JOHNSON,

ATTORNEYS AT LAW,

Office opposite Campbell Block,

TAMPA, FLORIDA.

WALL & TURMAN,

ATTORNEYS AT LAW,

Office in the Opera House,

TAMPA, FLORIDA.

S. M. SPARKMAN,　　　G. B. SPARKMAN,
State's Attorney.　　　Notary Public.

S. M. & G. B. SPARKMAN,

ATTORNEYS AT LAW

And Solicitors in Chancery,

Will practice in all the State Courts of South Florida and the United States Circuit and District for the Southern District of Florida.

LUCIUS FINLEY.　　　BARRON PHILLIPS.

FINLEY & PHILLIPS,

ATTORNEYS AT LAW,

Office in Henderson's Building.

TAMPA, FLORIDA.

HUGH C. MACFARLANE,

ATTORNEY AT LAW,

Office over Macfarlane & Cleaveland's Shoe Store,

TAMPA, FLORIDA.

WM. J. BERRY,

FIRST-CLASS TINNER.

Guttering and Roofing done in best style.

Ghira Building.

TAMPA, FLORIDA.

Write to this Agency for information on the best and cheapest route to this part of Florida. You can save money by it.

APPLY TO THIS AGENCY FOR ANYTHING REFERRING TO LAND OR INVESTMENTS.

If you want a home in Florida apply to this Agency. Facilities unsurpassed by any in the State.

JAS. H. BROWN.   J. GEDDIE FRASER.

BROWN & FRASER.
PLASTERERS,
TAMPA. FLORIDA.

Brick Work, Cementing and Kalsomining.

CORNICING ○ AND ○ ORNAMENTING ○ A ○ SPECIALTY.

Work done in any part of the State. All work guaranteed.

TAMPA LUMBER COMPANY,

Manufacturers of all kinds of

Fine * Lumber, * Brackets * and * Mouldings.

ALL KINDS OF FANCY WORK DONE.

——— FOREIGN AND HOME ORDERS SOLICITED. ———

NEW PAINT HOUSE,

JACKSON STREET, TAMPA, FLA.

A. B. McKENZIE, PROPRIETOR.

Has just received and will keep constantly on hand a full supply of paints, oils, glass, putty, varnishes and all painters' and glaziers' supplies. Orders for work in any kind of painting, varnishing, glazing and kalsomining will receive prompt attention. Estimates of any work furnished. Give us a call and work, and satisfaction guaranteed.

Write to this Agency for information on the best and cheapest route to this part of Florida. You can save money by it.

THE SOUTH FLORIDA RAILROAD.

This popular tourist route and important freight line connects Tampa with Jacksonville and the eastern coast of Florida, via the St. Johns river. Upon the southern shore of Lake Monroe, a portion of the St. Johns, is Sanford, the eastern terminus of the road in Orange county.

From Sanford the road runs in a southwesterly course to Tampa, 115 miles, passing through the most beautiful and productive section of South Florida. From the car window the tourist sees constant changes of landscape and new scenes of beauty, as he is whirled around and among the sparkling fresh water lakes that dot the entire surface of the country in Orange, Polk and Hillsborough counties. In Orange county are seen thriving orange groves and evidences of prosperity and thrift not equaled in any other place in the South.

Orange county is referred to as especially prosperous and thrifty, not because it is an older settled county, but because it has had for a longer time better transportation facilities than those enjoyed by the counties of Polk and Hillsborough further to the west; but the amazing strides that these two counties have made during the past year, since the South Florida Railroad has been opened to the Gulf of Mexico, give promise that at no distant future they will not only equal but outstrip their more advanced neighbor, Orange county, in the race for wealth.

The soil along the line of the road is sandy, but capable of an extraordinary production and is wonderfully responsive to cultivation and care. In the hammocks a deep and fertile soil is found, and there can be grown, without the aid of fertilizer, all the products that man can desire. While the line of the South Florida Railroad passes through this delightful scenery and these rich lands it is important, not alone for its local business and to those who dwell along the line, but it connects South Florida with the North and West by lines of steamers and rail, giving rapid and safe transportation to those who travel either for business or pleasure, and to the tender fruits and vegetables which are, by it, pushed forward, without delay, to the Northern and Western markets.

At Sanford a line of fast mail steamers connects with the fast mail trains of the South Florida Railroad, and makes the run in one night from Sanford to Jacksonville, there connecting with the fast mail trains of the Savannah, Florida and Western Railway, over the Atlantic Coast line for New York.

Within a few weeks an all rail outlet from Hillsborough county, Tampa and points on the line of the South Florida Railroad, will be opened via Lakeland, Gainesville and Savannah, reducing the time from Tampa to Savannah more than eight hours and taking the productions of the west coast of Florida, without reloading or change of cars, direct from Tampa to the ships side at Savannah; or, if rail transportation be preferred, to Philadelphia, Baltimore, New York and Boston. If a Western market is desired the same produce can be carried there without change, without delay—thus insuring to producers on the west coast the surest and quickest transportation known in the South.

All property along the line is rapidly increasing in value and the new towns and villages constantly springing up, give evidence that those who have settled in Florida have come to stay and make the State their future and permanent home. It is the policy of the South Florida Railroad to encourage immigration and settlement on the land near its line and to offer to those who come to build up the country all the inducements consistent with strict business principles. The road is first class in every respect, steel rails, a smooth road bed, first class equipment, air brakes, Janney couplers and platforms, heavy and powerful locomotives and a large corps of men on freight trains insures a rapid handling of freight, while careful management and strict orders and regulations guarantee that property shall be properly cared for and safely delivered at destination or to connecting lines. Passenger trains will compare favorably with those on the largest Northern roads and parlor cars give comfort and elegance to those desiring the luxury at a lower price than is generally charged for similar service elsewhere.

The principal towns along the line of the South Florida Railroad are Sanford, Longwood, Orlando, Kissimmee, Auburndale, Bartow, Lakeland, Plant City and Tampa. At Lakeland a branch of the South Florida Railroad extends north to Pemberton Ferry, there connecting with the Florida Southern Railroad which extends to Gainesville, at which point it connects with the Savannah, Florida and Western Railway, giving quick transportation to all points in the North, East, South and West. Telegraph offices are at all these stations named and visitors will find good hotels and ample accommodations at all seasons of the year. At Tampa, the western terminus of the road, connection is made with steamers (during the season) for Havana, Key West, New Orleans, Cedar Key and all points on the west coast. This is a favorite passenger line to Havana, as by taking it passengers avoid the long and tedious voyage from New York and save the miseries of sea sickness, making shorter time to Havana than by any other line. As an instance of the time to Havana, New York papers of Wednesday are delivered by this route, in Havana, on Sunday morning. At Tampa, connecting daily with the trains from Sanford, the fast and elegant steamer "Margaret" of the people's line (the same line that operates the fast mail service on the St. Johns river) makes daily trips to all points on Manatee river, that is: Palma Sola, Braidentown, Palmetto, Manatee and Ellenton, the great vegetable producing section of Florida, and she also stops at that Gem of the Gulf, Egmont Key. The sail down the Bay from Tampa to Manatee river is one that no traveler should miss; for the beauties of this trip are unexcelled in the United States, and the bay is said to equal in beauty the far-famed Bay of Naples.

Twice each week mail steamers leave Tampa for Key West, making the run to that noted city and returning the following day; thus bringing to Tampa from Key West and Havana the varied products of those tropical regions.

The health of the country through which the road passes, will not only compare favorably with other sections of the South, but the health statistics of the United States show that the percentage of deaths from sickness is smaller in Florida than in any other State in the Union. All the more violent forms of sickness known in the North, such as diphtheria, pneumonia, scarlet fever, etc., etc., are here unknown, and, by ordinary prudence, even the slightest case of chills and fever can be avoided.

For full particulars and information apply to,

FREDERICK H. RAND,

General Freight and Passenger Agent, S. F. R. R.,

SANFORD, FLORIDA.

www.ingramcontent.com/pod-product-compliance
Lightning Source LLC
Chambersburg PA
CBHW020858160426
43192CB00007B/981